How to Turn

YOUR DESIRES
AND IDEALS
INTO REALITY

➤— 2nd Edition —≪
Includes Detailed Testimonials

BROWN LANDONE

SUMNER M. DAVENPORT

Self-Investment Company, LLC

2060d E. Avenida de los Arboles #571

Thousand Oaks, Ca 91362

www.selfinvestmentpublishing.com

Graphics and Cover, Sumner M. Davenport © 2007, 2015

Research & Editing, Sumner M. Davenport © 2007, 2015

Published by Self-Investment Company, LLC © 2007, 2015

10 9 8 7 6 5 4 3 2

ISBN10: 0-9815238-2-x

ISBN 13: 978-0-9815238-2-8

Gratitude

*"At times our own light goes out and is rekindled
by a spark from another person.
Each of us has cause to think with deep gratitude of
those who have lighted the flame within us. "
~Albert Schweitzer~*

First of all, my thanks to Brown Landone for giving the world the original publication of this book. His personal experiences and research has opened the door to understanding for countess individuals over the years. Thank you to all the inspired "leaders" whose quotes are used throughout this book, and whose lives, works and words continue to inspire. Thank you to the contributors whose testimonials may assist others to learn from their experiences.

I thank my Source for everything in my life, my growth and my blessings. I thank all my teachers and guides, the sages and Angels in my daily life.

My thanks to my Grandfather, Everett Sumner Burbank, for his faith in me and his constant guidance. My thanks to

Whitney Challad for defining friendship. My love and thanks to Lancelot for sharing unconditional love. My love and thanks to Jack Epps for his quiet caring and for being a teacher of patience. My thanks to all my friends for their love and support and for being examples of living.

Thank you to Google^{TM} and Wikipedia, for helping me to find the quotes and the supporting information for this book.

Thank you to all the new readers of this book, and the changes they will make in their lives after reading and embodying the message, and whose ripples will make changes in the world for themselves and many others.

Sumner M. Davenport
Editor, Contributing Author

TABLE OF CONTENTS

Foreword

This book was originally published in the early 1900's. Some of the language or social examples may seem antiquated; however, humankind has not changed. We still have the same needs, desires, and dreams. In that truth, the substance and validity of this information is timeless.

There are many teachers in the world today, all delivering the same message in books, seminars and throughout the media. Countless people continue to flock to events and purchase numerous books in search of the answer to their burning question, "how can I change my life?" The message is not *new-age* as some will assert; it is ageless

My research shows that this message was first written about in 360AD, by Epictetus, then again in 1892, by Thomas J. Hudson, PhD, and again in 1905 by

Wallace D. Wattles and Annie Besant, and again1912 by Charles F. Haanel, and again in 1926 by RHJ, and again in1931 by Emmet Fox, and again in 1937 and 1945 by Napoleon Hill, and again in 1957 by Earl Nightingale, and again in 1964 by Maxwell Maltz, and again from 1968 - 1972 by Og Mandino, W. Clement Stone, Zig Ziglar, Brian Tracy and others, and by numerous additional authors over the years.

Most recently this message was sparked again by the movie, The Secret. This movie has sprouted another group of teachers all delivering the same message, clothed in their individual interpretation.

Some book publishers will take the works of an author now in the public domain and republish it as originally written without challenging the beliefs to current time and environment. We have taken this timeless message, tested it in today's society. When this edition was in its draft form, it was given to several people to "test". Some of their testimonials are placed in the book.

Preface

These current testimonials include as much detail as possible to show how their results were created. Their names and email addresses are used with permission unless they requested otherwise. We give credit to the original author and the new contributors.

As I continue to seek the answers to life, other inspirational and educational works from masters of the past back will be brought back into print. The updated edition of each book will include current day testimonials to support the messages. If you have a success testimonials to share that you would like considered for one of these upcoming books, you are welcomed to send it to the email address provided in the Testimonial Contributors section of this book.

Also strategically placed in this book are quotes from various authors and educators, past and present. These powerful change-makers have inspired me throughout the years and given light to hope and possibilities. They are each given an introduction in the Quote References section.

The message is consistent, and the teachers continually show up. It's a matter of finding the one that "speaks to you".

"When the pupil is ready, the teacher will appear."
~ Chinese proverb ~

Perhaps this book will be your teacher.

Wishing you continued success,
Sumner M. Davenport

Preface
From the original text

THE MAN WHO WORKED OUT THE PROCESS

It is unusual I assume for a businessman to accept the obligation of writing a foreword to a book of *Idealism*, and any attempt on my part to add to its spiritual content would be vain assumption. But since I know of the phenomenal results of *Idealizing* the process, I can perhaps give some measure of faith and hope to those who have not always succeeded and who now doubt the possibility of making their *Ideals* become realities.

My certainty of the results of this process bases itself upon many years' personal contact with the attainments of Brown Landone, upon my own individual and business success in using the process, and upon my intimate acquaintance with the many executives who have with his aid made their *Ideals* come true. Some of these *Ideals* have been of the higher things of life; some of more mundane affairs, such as increasing one's salary from two or three thousand a year to a thousand a month or more by a few weeks' use of the process.

Brown Landone, the man, like all of us, has his individual habits and hobbies known only to intimate friends. For instance, he never reads anything *Idealistic* immediately before going to sleep. "If I do," he says, "my mind reacts and I have unpleasant dreams; but, if I read something weird, my soul reacts and I live the night in a state of high spiritual consciousness."

Then there is the passion of "cleaning up things." Today, this is most annoying to some of the intimate friends whom he visits, for no sooner is he in the home than he makes for the basement or attic to satisfy his soul's desire to make things clean. It is a passion with him; it was born in him. As a child he would clean up his playroom rather than play with his toys. When but five years old he became so angry because the servants would not let him mop the kitchen floors that he ran away from home!

Although handicapped in childhood and youth with what most of us consider insurmountable physical handicaps, yet he has lived long, worked much and retains enduring vitality. Those in whose time he first worked - Helen Wilmans, Dr. Adams, Mrs. Eddy, Dr. Stockham and others -have long since passed into the greater life. Yet, today (I know from years of association), he often works twenty hours out of twenty-four and finds life and the work a joy because he loves both. You and I may not wish to work thus, yet it gives one great consciousness of power to know that someone has attained such spiritual contact with Life that he is able to do so.

His recreation is painting. After a day's work, usually from eighteen to twenty hours, he paints to rest himself before going to sleep. He paints at such times with phenomenal rapidity.

He has worked much and all he has done or written is original. In point of fact, he has done so many original things that many find it difficult to keep track of his work. More than twenty years ago (1920) he wrote of the value of vitamins, now being accepted by the medical profession; a generation ago he proved the solar plexus to be a brain by itself, a statement then ridiculed by biologists but now accepted; seventeen years ago (1923) he discovered that tone is most resonantly projected on the parabolic curve and it is just now being used by engineers to secure valuable talents; within this decade he has formulated a new science of sociology which conservative

French thinkers have called "epoch making." He was the first man to work out a new science of the arts unifying the basic principles of music, literature, painting, sculpture and architecture; to work out neural reaction; and to prove that new brain structure can be developed by conscious functioning just as Burbank proved that new plant structures can be developed.

Preface

In this book one thought deserves more than passing mention. During the centuries philosophers have sought the basis of the soul's faith in the unity of all things. Clearly to present that basis of unity is now, I know, Brown Landone's one great life aim. He may or may not succeed in making the world conscious of this unity, but at least the attempt in The Spirit of Matter comes nearer making us know that the spiritual and material world are one than anything written previously. With such a consciousness of the unity of all things of spirit and of matter, the faith is strong and the way is clear to make our *Ideals* come true.

EDGAR H. FELIX - New York City, June, 1922

***

DESIRE, IDEALS AND REALITIES

How To Turn Your Desires and Ideals Into Reality

CHAPTER 1

WHAT DESIRES CAN YOU MAKE COME TRUE?

Every desire is the heart of some *Ideal*. Your desires always come true. Your wishes seldom do; they die by consuming themselves in forever wishing wishes. A desire with a body or an *Ideal* with a heart always becomes a reality! Every desire is the heart center of some *Ideal* that is either revealed to consciousness and understood or hidden in the ultra-consciousness and misunderstood. The *Ideal* is the active body of the desire. Do not expect your desire to come true unless you give it a body. Construct an *Ideal* that gives substance to each desire. Make the *Ideal* active; endow it with the process of attainment. Then, it will become a reality! It will come true!

Desire
de·sire, noun
1. a longing or craving

Ideal
i·de·al, noun
1. a perfect image in the mind
2. the substance of things that come true

Wish
verb
1. a want, usually associated with the hope
of magic for its attainment
(dictionary.com)

But an "idea" is not an "*Ideal*"! That is where your trouble often lies! Only a few - a very, very few - of your ideas ever come true. And very, very few of your thoughts and plans ever materialize if they are made up of ideas instead of *Ideals*. **An *Ideal* always manifests itself in action and becomes a reality**. Unless it does so, it is not an *Ideal*.

In using the term "*Ideal*" I am not conceiving any particular meaning of the word to fit my own philosophy;

I am using the word as it is made definite by all dictionaries of the English language, that is, that *an Ideal is a perfect image in the mind*. An *Ideal* differs from an idea. An idea is an image in the mind. An *Ideal* is a *perfect* image in the mind. Every idea or *Ideal* is composite; it is made up of parts. Your *idea* of an orange includes, among a score of images: certain images of *color*, for you know it is not black; certain images of *size*, for you know an orange is not as small as a pinhead or as large as a watermelon; certain images of *odor*, it does not smell like an onion; and certain images of *taste*, for it does not taste like carrots or potatoes, pickles or chili-sauce.

An idea is imperfect because it lacks mind images which it should include and because it includes images which should not be included. Your idea of a certain person is imperfect because your idea of them does not include all the imaged qualities a perfect human should possess and includes imaged qualities that the perfect human should not manifest. But your perfect *Ideal* of a person includes all of those qualities that such a person should possess and none of those, which they should not manifest.

An idea is not perfect; it is but a partial image, and lacking that something which is essential, seldom comes true. Usually the element an idea lacks is the very element that, if the idea possessed it, would make the idea manifest as a reality.

Differing from an idea, an *Ideal* is a perfect image in the mind. It includes all of the component parts that it should include and it includes nothing that it should not include. Thus, in content and substance, it is perfect. *Ideals* are the substance of things that come true. Ideas are but mental skeletons; they are without heart and body. They have no desire, no *Ideal*.

Desire may be related to an idea or it may not. It is never a part of it. That is one of the elements an idea lacks. An *Ideal* has always a heart of desire. That is one of the reasons why *Ideals* come true. Mere ideas do not thrill the soul, urging and forcing man to action. *Ideals*, surging with desire and impelling to action, lead man to live, serve, sacrifice and die that his *Ideals* may be made manifest as realities.

Your ideas seldom materialize. They lack desire and impulse to action. *Ideals* always come true. **Change your ideas into *Ideals* and they will become realities.** It is easy for you to do so as soon as you know what it is the idea lacks. Thoughts formed of *Ideals* become realities, as surely as though they were conceived directly by Divine Spiritual Source, Itself.

Which of your *Ideals* can you make come true? Not one of them if they exist only as desires, for desire is but the soul's impulse to become real! But, give a desire a spiritual body, that is, embody it in an *Ideal*, and it will always come true! For *Ideals* are substance of things that are!

"If you greatly desire something,
have the guts to stake everything on obtaining it."
~ Brendan Francis ~

CHAPTER 2

CAN YOU, YOURSELF, MAKE YOUR IDEALS BECOME REALITIES?

Some of you are endowed with faith and some beset with doubt. Of those endowed with faith based upon spiritual knowledge, there is not one whose faith is not weakened a little by trifling doubts. Of those beset with the darkest of doubts, there is not one whose doubt is not enlightened a little by a touch of faith.

When I state that *Ideals* come true none of you deny it or think of denying it. But, when I assure you that every *Ideal* always comes true and that every one of your own particular *Ideals* can be changed to a material reality, my

28

statement contrasts so astoundingly with your past experiences of having tried faithfully to attain that which you desire, that some of you feel it can not be true; some of you may doubt even my common sense in making such an assertion. You, who doubt that every *Ideal* comes true, doubt sincerely; doubt, because of common sense judgments based upon your present knowledge. No matter what the cause, doubt interferes with your realization of your *Ideals*. It dampens the fire of desire and lessens your effort to attain that which you wish because you think the effort is useless.

I do not wish you to accept any statement; I wish you to know truth! Do not change from doubt to blind belief; it will do you no permanent good, blind faith soon dies. But what are the "ideas" in your mind that make you doubt?

First, mistaking *ideas* for **Ideals.**

Second, your idea of the density of matter.

Third, your idea of the solidity of matter.

Fourth, your idea of matter as motionless and lifeless.

Fifth, your present incomplete knowledge of the process of making *Ideals* become realities.

These are the only serious causes of doubt; five stones in the path of faith and attainment. I shall not, in succeeding Chapters, give them more attention than they deserve, but just enough to remove them.

By and large, your doubt is based upon the seeming impossibility of etheric images of the mind being able easily to change, re-form and re-create the substance of matter that is seemingly so dense, solid and lifeless. If you could know that matter is not as dense as it seems, not as solid as it appears, not as lifeless as it is assumed to be; if you could know these things, then doubt would be faith and faith would be divinely certain, forever lasting, and ever impelling to action.

Most of your trouble, then, relates to your idea of the nature of matter, its substance and attributes. In what follows I shall not be so silly as to assert that matter does not exist, that it is a mere claim of matter, or that it is an illusion.

If I should assert that matter is non-existent, you could laugh at me and justly, for I am so conscious of the existence of matter that I find it necessary to have a house in which to live, a bed in which to sleep, clothes to wear and food to eat. If I should assert that matter is a mere claim of being matter, I would corner myself; when people owe me money, I am not content with the claim, I prefer the money itself. If I should state that matter is an "illusion of the mind," you could, knowing the certainty of the law that only like perceives like, smile to yourself over the idea that nothing but an illusionary mind could conceive an illusionary world, eat illusionary vegetables, wear illusionary shirts, handle illusionary money, use and depend upon ten thousand illusionary things and live upon an illusionary earth.

I hold that matter is existent and that it is very unwise and detrimental to deny its existence and attempt to live up to the denial, for instance to deny the existence of material food and try to live without it. But, I hold also that it is lack of knowledge of the true nature of matter that makes us think of it as dense, solid, motionless and lifeless.

If in our greater knowledge of matter we find that it is only energy in reality, that it is not restricted energy but infinite energy, and that it is of the same substance as spirit, then our concept of matter becomes so like our concept of the substance of which *Ideals* are made, that it is possible for us to perceive some definite connection, a real relation, perhaps a similarity, perhaps even a co-existence of the substance of every *Ideal* and the substance of every material reality.

With such knowledge found in next succeeding Chapters, our faith that *Ideals* come true, because they are of the same substance as matter, can be and is justified. Such faith will fire anew our *Ideals* and desires and impel us to cease no effort until they become realities; and with knowledge of the process of attainment, we shall know by experience that it is not as difficult as it once seemed. And you, yourself, can make your *Ideals* become realities.

Faith is the substance of things hoped for. *Ideals* are the substance of the things that are.

"To one who has faith, no explanation is necessary.

To one without faith, no explanation is possible."

~ St. Thomas Aquinas ~

TESTIMONIAL:
I FINALLY UNDERSTOOD THE DIFFERENCE

"For years I have taken classes and read books about identifying what you desire and how to have it. It seemed like it didn't matter what I did or did not do, my results were always the same and disappointing. When I read through this book the first time, I felt something inside, like a deeper awareness of the answer I was seeking. Then I read it a second time and began to see the difference between my ideas and my Ideals.

My ideas were many times a fleeting thought with contradictory thoughts in between. I would have an idea of my desire and follow that with all the ideas of limitations. My reactions to consistently not getting my desired results would be similar to a spoiled child who demanded something without having earned it.

My Ideals are more of a real commitment. A commitment to the complete desire and everything required. When I would list my desires in the past, it was a longing or a wishing feeling.

When I made the commitment to Idealize like Landone describes in Chapter 8; and reprogram my body and thought process to see, taste, feel and touch every part of my desire as already being real, my results changed almost miraculously." ~ Terry Bessel, Austin, TX.~

THE SPIRIT
OF MATTER

How To Turn Your Desires and Ideals Into Reality

CHAPTER 3

WHAT COMPACTNESS OF MATTER GIVES TO YOUR IDEALS

Your ideas are always changing and you are ever changing your attitude regarding them. Why? They have no form, no body of spiritual substance; being without body, they are notions and very changeable notions at that.

But you are loyal to your *Ideals*; you are steadfast in your allegiance to them. Why? Because there is something fixed and real about them; they are made of spiritual substance; they are the actual bodies of your desires; of your highest *Ideals*, you say that they are fixed as the stars, by which you mean that they are made of substance that is eternal.

You hold steadfastly to your *Ideals*; but, since *Ideals* are of the spiritual and etheric substance, can you easily change them into material actualities, make them manifest in a world of matter which appears so compact and dense? This idea that matter is compact and hence dense is one of the stones in the path of faith; as an idea, it prevents you from making sufficient effort to make your *Ideals* come true. When you study matter as it is, as the great physical scientists now know it, and when you find that that which is called density is but the compactness of materially empty space, etheric substance, spiritual substance, does it not open up new visions?

Already you perceive that, if so-called density of matter is but compactness of etheric substance, that which makes density possible is similar to and co-existent with the very substance in which *Ideals* exist and of which they are made. All of which suggests that

40

that which appears to us as density is of aid in giving substance to *Ideals*, in giving them bodies so that they can come true.

What is density of matter? If matter is dense, it must be compact, for the idea of density depends upon the idea of compactness. Is matter a compact substance? Read carefully and think; for this, to you, is vital. It means either that you can and will make your *Ideals* come true, or that you will slip through life forever wishing that you might have done so.

Matter, we say, employing terms in general use, is made up of masses, masses of minute particles, each particle of millions of molecules, each molecule of atoms, and each atom of from hundreds of thousands to millions of electrons. There is but one form of structure in the universe; the universe is the uni-verse, the creation of one law.

The moon is 2 thousand miles in diameter, but it is 240 thousand miles away from the earth; 2 units of matter, 240 units of etheric space. Our earth is 8 thousand miles in diameter, but it is 93,000 thousand miles from the sun; 8 units of matter, 93,000 units of etheric space. The sun's diameter is less than 1 million miles, but its nearest star-neighbor is more than 25,000 million miles away; 1 unit of matter, 25,000 units of etheric space. The materially empty etheric space - distance between any two heavenly bodies is infinitely greater than the size of either. Thus it is throughout the universe. Thus it is throughout matter. The material emptiness of the universe is a true indication of the so-called density of matter.

What is the density of the molecule? A molecule is composed of atoms infinitely smaller than itself. Its atoms, however, are not close together; it is no more compact nor dense than the space of the heavens.

What is a molecule? Image the sun; image the Earth, Mars, Mercury, the other planets and their moons, all whirling and circling around the sun center to form our solar system. The system is a gigantic sphere. Of what?

Of nothing but etheric space. There is no shell to this sphere; it is just ether, conceived as a globe, within which whirl a few comparatively small specks of dust, the earth and the sun, for instance.

Look up in the air above you. Imagine the outline of a toy balloon without any material except a few specks of invisible dust in the space you image as a globe. That is the density of the universe; it is also as dense as the molecule that is merely an etheric globular space in which atoms, far, far apart, whirl around an etheric center.

Is not the density of matter already evaporating so that in it you see no hindrance to making your *Ideals* into realities? If not the molecule, is the atom dense? The atom, like the molecule, has no shell or body. It is merely a spherical system of ether space in which electrons whirl around an etheric center. So far nothing but infinite space and infinite energy in space! In such, what hindrance is there to your *Ideals* and desires coming true?

Is it, then, the electron that gives matter its appearance of density? Of course, if the electron were itself of good size and if its own substance were compact, it could give to matter some semblance of material density.

What is the size of the electron? Out of paper cut a square inch surface. Then imagine a tiny paper bag the size of a cubic inch. If this cubic inch box were filled with any one of several different gases, the space would contain approximately 441,000,000,000,000,000,000 molecules. They are very far apart; hence there is plenty of room in this cubic inch for a million times the number already given. Since each of these molecules is composed of atoms, each atom must be definitely smaller than the molecule. Since in an atom there are millions of electrons with comparatively great intervening spaces capable of holding millions more, how small, then, is the electron! You cannot conceive its infinite minuteness for, although each atom is but one-hundredth of one-millionth of one inch in diameter, the electron is fifty thousand times smaller than the atom!

Of course, you cannot imagine this; it is infinitely small, a part of the infinity of Divine Spiritual Source! And what is the electron?

Of what substance is it? All scientists agree that it is an infinitely small etheric whirl of energy, a whirling hole in space!

What then is density? Density is the spirit of matter, the infinite etheric energy-space of Divine Spiritual Source. It is that in which all things live and move and have their being. It exists between the infinitely small whirling electrons but a billionth of an inch from one another; it exists between whirling stars and infinitely large suns thousands of millions of millions of miles apart.

There is no density of matter to hinder the manifestation of your *Ideals* and desires. Since you, your *Ideals* and desires are of Divine Spiritual Source, and since the cells of your body and also the substance of all other material actualities are but the infinite energy-space of Divine Spiritual Source, certainly your *Ideals* composed of this substance, the only substance that exists, can and will and do come true. In fact, this etheric energy-space substance, which makes matter seem to be dense, is the very substance that gives bodies to your *Ideals* and thus makes them manifest in material actuality.

"The energy of the mind

is the essence of life."

~ Aristotle ~

CHAPTER 4

WHAT ATTRACTIVE MATTER OF ENERGY GIVES TO YOUR DESIRES

Another stone in the path of faith and the attainment of your *Ideals* and desires is the idea that matter is solid. As density was found to be but infinite energy space, the spiritual substance in which *Ideals* and all things exist, what will solidity turn out to be when you come to know it as it is?

Iron seems to be a solid substance and very hard. Does its hardness reside in matter or is it due to the spirit or energy of matter? The molecules and atoms of iron are no harder or more solid than the molecules and atoms of butter. Yet, it is difficult to drive a nail into a piece of iron and easy to drive one into a chunk of butter. That which makes it difficult to drive a nail into iron is the degree of attractive force existing between the particles. It is this force that holds molecules and their respective atoms to each other. When you drive a nail into iron, what you overcome is the attractive force that tries to prevent the molecules being pushed apart. It is easy to force apart the molecules of butter to make space for a nail. In this case also, what you overcome is the attractive force that holds together the molecules and atoms of butter.

When the degree of attractive force is comparatively great, we say the matter is hard and solid. When it is smaller, we say the matter is not hard and not so solid. But it is not matter itself that is solid or not solid. In truth, solidity is but the spirit of matter. It is another manifestation, the infinite attractive energy found throughout the universe. It is as infinite as Divine Spiritual Source. Matter is not solid! There is only one solid thing in the universe, the infinite attractive energy of

Divine Spiritual Source, which holds all things together. Your *Ideals* are of spirit. If you wish to change any part of your body, know that it is no more solid than the heavens; know that that which makes it appear solid and holds the tiny centers of force together, is but infinite attractive spirit; that this attractive spirit or energy is of Divine Spiritual Source, and is infinite.

Your soul, with its mind, love and life forces, is also of Divine Spiritual Source. Being direct of Divine Spiritual Source, made in His Image, you are supreme. Being supreme, your soul controls its *Ideals* and their actualities. Do not deny evil; that which we call evil exists, but when you know its real nature you find it is good. The solidity, which you feared as an evil hindrance to the manifestation of your desires and *Ideals*, is infinite attractive spirit, the very force that gives your desires the power to attract all that is necessary to make them come true.

"Go confidently in the direction of your dreams! Live the life you've imagined. As you simplify your life, the laws of the universe will be simpler."

~ Henry David Thoreau ~

CHAPTER 5

WHAT MOVEMENT IN MATTER GIVES TO YOUR BODY OF DESIRE

Ideals are of the substance of spirit and space; they have motion and life. Can they, then, manifest in matter if it be motionless and lifeless? That which lives has motion of itself and within itself; that which has such motion is not dead. All atoms are reservoirs of limitless energy. I use radium for illustration only because you have heard of it and know it. A grain of radium is a very small particle; it is less than one four-hundredth of one little ounce of matter. Yet, during every single second of time, a grain of radium gives off 2,000 impulses of energy.

Is this energy of the spirit? If it is of the spirit, it is enduring. Man's body sustained by the energy of the soul may last a hundred years. How long does atomic energy last? After one four-hundredth part of an ounce of radium has given off 2,000 impulses of energy every second of every hour of every day for 1,700 years, it has used up but part of its energy and has enough left to continue the process at the same rate for 1,700 years more, and then at a slower rate to continue forever. Spirit energy has power; has atomic energy power. If we knew how to free at one time all the energy of but one ounce of radium, its freed energy could toss all the navies of the world from the mid-Atlantic to the Mississippi Valley. What infinite energy there is in every atom of so-called matter! This energy is not of dead matter; it is the infinite energy of Divine Spiritual Source, in every atom!

All so-called matter is alive. It is alive with energy. It is Divine Spiritual Source, in manifestation. And, it moves! It moves within itself! An airplane flying 660 miles an hour would make us gasp! The earth whirls around the sun with incredible speed, 66,000 miles an hour! But a freed electron whizzes through space at the rate of 660,000,000 miles an hour! And such an electron can change its position 40,000,000 times while you are saying o-n-e! Every cell of your body is composed of billions of electrons pulsating and throbbing with energy and life! Every material of your body, brain, muscle, heart, and bone is composed of billions of cells, how many only the Creator knows. And every one of these cells is a gigantic and colossal universe of atoms of titanic force and electrons of infinite energy! Their energy waits for your soul to use it! Whatever part of your body you wish to change, can be changed, for matter is neither dense, nor solid, nor motionless, nor lifeless.

The same electrons, these same whirling centers of infinite energy, compose every form of matter: wood, and all things made of wood; iron, and all things of iron;

brass and gold; materials of all kinds; every thing you can see and touch and all other things! The substance of all things, *Ideals* and realities, is ever the same! All are of Divine Spiritual Source! *Ideals* can come true: all things can be changed, for the density of matter is but infinite energy space, the substance of all things; the solidity of matter is but the infinite attractive force of Divine Spiritual Source; and matter has motion and life moving at a tremendous rate responsive to the supreme energies of the soul, mind, love and life.

Can anyone, now knowing that the particles of seemingly motionless matter can move at a rate of 660,000,000 miles an hour and can change position 40,000,000 times in a second, doubt that it is this infinite energy of Divine Spiritual Source, in all things that gives to *Ideals* the possibility of manifesting as material actualities?

Matter so throbbing with energy and movement cannot hinder your *Ideals* coming true; but your idea of matter as dense, solid and motionless can hinder them by deadening your desire and lessening your effort. Change your idea of matter to a true *Ideal* of matter. For desires embodied in *Ideals*, in bodies of etheric substance possessing infinite energy, always come true! You cannot prevent them more than you can stop the whizzing of electrons or the whirling of stars.

"Spiritual energy flows in

and produces effects in the phenomenal world"

~ William James ~

DESIRE AND
IDEALS
AND
THE PROCESS
OF BECOMING
REALITIES

CHAPTER 6

THE ONLY THREE ACTIVITIES NECESSARY

First, there is the *Ideal* of Something Desired; Second, the Process that Leads to Attaining It; and Third, the Act of Making the Reality Yours.

These are the three basic activities of attaining that which you desire; they are the only ones which have been and can be successfully used in attaining any quality or degree of development within yourself or in obtaining any thing, condition or position in society or the world about you. These three activities are simply stated because they are true, not because I write them. Basic truths are always simple; and, if not enveloped in a mass of superfluous words or intertwined with a web of entangled thoughts, they are always easily understood. When simply stated and easily understood, it is easy to apply them.

If you permit your *Ideal* to be lost in a jungle of many words and your process to be misdirected by a multitude of varying thoughts and feelings, each pointing in a different direction, why, then, of course, your *Ideal* will not and cannot become a reality. Unless you can clearly and definitely state your *Ideal*, it is not sufficiently concrete to make any process of attaining it successful. Unless you can definitely and simply state what you are to do and how you are to do it, your plan of the process of attaining or obtaining that which you want will be confused and your effort will be partly wasted and probably unsuccessful.

Attaining that which you desire is easy and certain:

(1) if you conceive a clear-cut *Ideal* of what you desire

(2) if you turn the *Ideal* to the particular process that always leads to attaining or obtaining that which you wish; and

(3) if you know how to make the reality a part of you or your surroundings.

That you may know how to make your ideas and desires become realities, I now take up the process in this next section:

"All who have accomplished great things
have had a great aim;
have fixed their gaze on a goal which was high,
one which sometimes seemed impossible."
~ *Orison Swett Marden* ~

CHAPTER 7

TO ATTAIN YOUR DESIRES, ALL THREE MUST BE USED

If you *Idealize* and use all three of the basic activities and only those three, it is easy to make your *Ideals* become realities. You always attain when you *Idealize* and use them; but, if you leave out any one of the three, you fail to attain your desire, and no one can be blamed except yourself.

If you *Idealize* only that which you desire and hold faithfully to that *Ideal*; that is, if you use only the first of the three activities, you will succeed and justly in proportion to what you do.

Since Divine Spiritual Source, is justice, the result corresponds to the effort. *Idealizing* what you want and holding faithfully to the *Ideal* for months and even years brings you the success your effort merits, even after years you will still be holding to the *Ideal*.

And, if you *Idealize* that which you desire and attempt to take possession of it mentally, using the first and third of the three basic activities, you succeed and justly in proportion to what you do.

If, when in New York, you learn of a football game to be played in Boston and desire to be present, the *Ideal* of the *Thing Desired* is to be in Boston. If you desire to drive by automobile from New York to Boston that is the *Ideal* of the Process you intend to use to get to Boston. If you go to your garage and sit in your car for a day, a month or a year, holding faithfully all the time to the Thing Desired and holding also a mental picture of being in Boston, mentally picturing the first and third steps, but omitting the second one, before the year passes your friends will wish to send you to the madhouse; and only because you failed to use the second activity, that of the process of actually starting the machine and driving from New York to Boston.

It is not enough to hold *Ideals* of the *Thing Desired*, the first step. It is not sufficient and it may be dangerous to declare mentally that you possess it, the third step. It is not enough even to have faith that your desire will come true, though faith is the substance of things hoped for. You must put your *Ideals* into *Idealized* action for *Ideals* are the substance of things that are and *Idealized* action is the only certain process of attainment.

"Faith without works is dead" does not stand-alone; Christ and the apostles presented the truth many times: "I must work the works of Him that sent Me. . . . Return to Divine Spiritual Source, and do works. What doth it profit though a man say he hath faith, and have not works? Can faith save him? Was not Abraham, our father, justified by works? By works was faith made perfect. I will give unto every one of you according to your works. He that overcometh and keepeth my works unto the end, to him will I give power over the nations." Of the names to be written in the Book of Life, they are to be judged" according to their works"; and the very last message, last Chapter of Revelation, is "Behold, I come quickly; and my reward is with me, to give every man according as his work shall be."

"Hitch your wagon to a STAR" is not sufficient." "HITCH your wagon to a star" brings results."

"Positive thinking by itself does not work.
Your embodied vision, partnered with vibrant
thinking, harmonized with active listening, and
supported with your conscious action
- will clear the path for your Miracles."
~ Sumner M. Davenport ~

CHAPTER 8

HOW TO FORM AN IDEAL THAT WILL COME TRUE

First, an *Ideal* to come true must be an *Ideal*; an *idea* will not do. Second, an *Ideal* to become a reality must have a heart of desire, and a good strong heart. Third, an *Ideal* to come into manifestation must be a body of real etheric substance. Fourth, an *Ideal* to become an actuality must possess an impulse of action. Lacking any one or more of these, your *Ideal* do not become realities.

First your *Ideal* must be an *Ideal*, not an idea. The *Ideal* will come true. Since most people think and plan in ideas; their thoughts and plans seldom materialize: After repeated failures, some become discouraged, despondent or resigned and some lose faith in their capacity to attain the great goal and doubt the justice of society, the world and Divine Spiritual Source. Other men and women think in *Ideal*; with them it is a habit. Such men and women are successful and attain to a great extent that which they desire. They attain in proportion to their *Ideal*.

You may *Idealize* your thoughts of ethical and spiritual advancement and attain soul consciousness; yet when it comes to other matters you may use only ideas and fail. On the other hand, although others may not *Idealize* ethical and spiritual concepts as you do, yet they do *Idealize*, that is, **make perfect images** of their thoughts of development, advancement, work, and business; and hence they succeed in those lines to a greater extent than you do. This is just; in fact, it is Divine Spiritual Source's justice. You fail in that which you do not *Idealize*; you succeed in that which you *Idealize*. They also fail in that which they do not *Idealize* and succeed in that in which they use *Ideals*.

67

Back of every *thing* in the world there is an *Ideal*: back of the design of every chair; the decoration of every room; the cut and material of every gown and every suit of clothes; back of every thing that ever comes true. Those who think in little *Ideals* succeed in little things; those who think in big *Ideals* succeed in big things.

No advance of mankind has ever been effected except it was first formed by *Ideals* of some kind: no painting was ever painted, no statue ever sculptured, no music ever composed, except first conceived as *Ideal*. No motor, no dynamo, no engine, no printing press, no linotype, no automobile, no airplane, not one was ever invented except it first existed as an *Ideal*. Nothing in education was ever taught and no ethical or spiritual concept was ever preached that did not previously exist in *Ideal* form in the mind.

Those who think ideas never attain to greatness. Great men and women always think in *Ideals.* Change your "ideas" to "*Ideals!*" How? By making it a perfect image, adding desire, giving it body substance, and creating in it an irresistible impulse to manifest itself in action.

How can you complete an idea so as to make it an *Ideal*? First, by adding the factors the idea lacks. You have an idea of the color of an apple. How perfect is it? Take paints and try to paint a picture of an apple and you will discover that there are scores of tints and blends of colors that your idea does not contain. You have an idea of the profile of the face of someone you love. Take a pencil and try to draw that profile! You have an idea of the shape and form of the legs of your table. Close your eyes; run your fingers over one of the legs; feel every indentation, every part that projects, the number of rings around the legs. Scores of new factors are added to your idea.

How can you be certain that you have added everything the perfect image ought to contain and left out everything the image should not contain? Although there are many millions of degrees of variation and an unlimited number of combinations, there are but a few different basic qualities that enter into our images. They are: colors, sounds, tastes, odors, movements and directions of movement, balance or lack of balance, fineness or roughness, hardness or softness, heat or cold, lightness or heaviness.

Take any idea you wish to come true. Image it in your mind as it now is, an imperfect idea. Then, take the factor of colors. Image it again, mentally seeing every color it has possessed, does possess or could possess. In this same way go over the idea of that which you desire. Use every one of the elements of color, sound, taste, odor, heat, cold, motion, direction of motion, form, size, balance, fineness, roughness, hardness, softness, lightness, heaviness.

Do not leave out a single one. When you have finished you will have the form of a perfect image, of an *Ideal*, but it will still be only the form, without a heart of desire, without an etheric body, and without impulse to impel action.

Next, add desire!

"Nothing great in the world has been accomplished

without passion."

~ George Wilhelm Friedrich Hegel ~

CHAPTER 9

FIRING THE HEART-DESIRE OF YOUR IDEAL

Wishes are but wishes; they lead only to wishing more wishes. Desires are heartbeats of soul; they demand and impel to action. A wish turns ever to itself, wishing that something will come to make itself true. A desire goes out from self; it daringly reaches out, demanding the thing desired, and divinely creates it in reality.

Put the following truths together: Desire is the heart of your *Ideal*; in this heart are the fires of attainment; sometimes they die down and are dim; sometimes they burn brightly and glow with hope and set fire to action; unless they thus burn with the light of hope and the fire of action, your *Ideal* will not come true. When the fires of desire are dimmed by disappointments or discouragement, or memories of the failures of the past, what are you going to do about it? **Feed the fires with your feelings and emotions**! Your thoughts will not do; they are but damp wood and wet sand. Desires are of the heart; they cannot be made to burn brightly by adding ideas and thoughts of the mind.

Is it a thing, material thing, you have desired and for which desire burns low because of past failures to attain it, or is it a new desire that dares not burn brightly for fear of disappointment should it not be attained? Fire your desire so that it will come true. Fire it with YOUR feelings and emotions.

Are you a young woman and is it a dainty rose-colored gown you desire? Image the color of it and feel the joy of gowning yourself in that color. Feel the pleasure it would give you to look at yourself in that color. Think of its color again, -the color of roses. Imagine that you have perfumed the gown with just a touch of essence of roses. Feel the joy of smelling the sweet odor of roses. Feel the joy of smelling the perfume with which your dress is scented. Think of the feel of the material, how soft and delicate. Feel the joy you feel in feeling it. Think of the lightness of the dress. Feel the joy you experience in handling light and dainty and fluffy things. Feel the joy you would feel in putting on that dress and in waiting for your sweetheart to call. Feel the joy you would feel as he admired it and complimented you upon it. Feel the joy you would feel dressed in that gown, when with a group of people. Is not your desire fired and burning with impulse to act? Will you not do something to get that dress; and, *Idealizing* your doing you will do it in the right way and get it in the right way.

Do you a young man desire a new suit of clothes? Fire your desire with your feelings. Image the suit you wish, its color, cut, form, material, and fit to you. Feel how happy you would feel dressed in that suit calling on the girl you love. Feel how proud you would feel if you

74

could wear it when going home to see mother. Feel how satisfied you would feel walking into the office dressed in that suit. Feel all your good feelings, felt under all other conditions, in relation to that suit. Is not your desire fired to the point where you will do something to get it and, *Idealizing* your doing, you will do the right thing and get it in the right way?

Is it a position you desire? Feel the joy the income of that position would give you. Feel the pleasures you could obtain with that income. Feel the joy of the opportunities the income would give. Feel the true pride of advancement. Feel the joy of knowing you have attained the position and made good. Feel the joy of generously helping others when in that position. Feel what that position would mean to you among your fellows. Feel what it would mean to you among businessmen. Feel all these feelings, feeding your desires with your FEELINGS instead of with wishes and thoughts, and you will do something to attain that which you desire.

Think, think, think of wishes and you will live a nervous wreck and die in the mental madhouse of unfulfilled mental desires. Feed the desires of your *Ideals* with your own feelings and emotions, and the higher the feelings and emotions, the stronger the fire and your desires will turn to action that cannot be prevented. And since your desires are hearts of *Ideals*, that which you do will be right.

"To desire is to obtain."

~ James Allen ~

TESTIMONIAL:
I WASN'T WORTHY TO HAVE WHAT I DESIRED

"My life appeared to be one disappointment after another. I desired a joyful life, yet it appeared that everything seemed against my having it. I wrote lists, I did affirmations, I read books and attended seminars all in an effort to find out what more I needed to do. I got deeper in debt, gained weight and lost relationships.

When I read this book, and initially started Idealizing, I found myself procrastinating and not following through with the complete process. With each procrastination, I had a deep feeling of defeat and hopelessness.

One day, when taking with a Coach I tearfully admitted that I was not worthy of the life I desired. I had been molested as a child and no one came to my defense. In fact my Mother who I depended on as my protector, turned her back and actually blamed me for the incident. I was told I was disgusting and that I should have fought harder if I didn't want it. In a home where love was limited, I was accused of letting my self be

77

molested as a way to be special. I was only 8 years old and the accusations and blame rooted deep. Later as a teenager I was again raped. By then I believed what I had been told years earlier so I must have deserved it. As a young woman I was starved for love and acceptance. I dated and worked for men who consistently told me I was unworthy of whatever I was asking for, whether it was love, a raise or respect. Sharing my past with someone usually resulted in my pain being used to manipulate me or humiliate me. All these actions kept affirming that I was damaged and unworthy. My feelings of being undeserving of love and respect does not relieve these men of the responsibility of their abusive behaviors.

As an adult, I could logically say that I was not to blame for what happened to me as a child, and it should not effect me as an adult. As a logically thinking person I could say that I was deserving, but deep inside of me was the contradiction.

For years I sought help to find my strength and self respect and I made progress, yet the underlying feeling of unworthiness still haunted me. My life felt like an ongoing struggle and disappointment.

I made a commitment to doing whatever it took to make positive changes in my life. I wrote out my Ideal in every detail as Mr. Landone describes. To begin with I had to have an Ideal of a worthy child. Me, the worthy child.

In chapter 8, Mr. Landone says to image it in your mind as it now is - an imperfect idea. Then Idealize it by seeing it transform into the perfection. I saw myself as a hurt and disappointed child. I Idealized an Angelic layer of protection around me. I had difficulty Idealizing that the rape didn't happen, so I Idealized myself getting all the support and love I needed to heal from the trauma. I Idealized hearing the adults around me telling me that I was loved and cherished. I heard their voices tell me that the man would never hurt me again, that I could again trust adults. I saw the adults support me and send the man away. I felt the tears of feeling loved and feeling safe roll down my cheeks. I Idealized myself growing up with these feelings of being loveable and being loved.

I Idealized myself laughing and people laughing with me. As Mr. Landone says, I used every one of the elements of color, sound, taste, odor, heat, cold, motion, direction of motion, form, size, balance, fineness, roughness, hardness, softness, lightness, heaviness. I created my Ideal childhood and my young formative years. I wrote it out like a story.

This took me a about a week to get a clear Ideal, but when I did, it grew even more on its own. As I developed this Ideal, I got excited about it. To help me in the creating process I found one baby picture of myself laughing, and another as a small girl. Then I found pictures in magazines of happy families. I put my face in the pictures. Looking at these pictures gave me a visual to help fuel my mental image.

I did not tell anyone I was doing this. There was still a part of me in the beginning that said I was crazy, I couldn't change the past, and I didn't need anyone else to confirm that thought. I wasn't changing the past, but in the light of my adult understanding, I was changing the emotions I had attached to the past. I was creating the Ideal energy of being worthy of a joy filled life.

I also had the Ideal for the results I wanted in my life now. I found it easier to Idealize my job, my weight and my relationships. Anytime I started to feel unworthy I would Idealize my perfect childhood. I would look at the happy photos and family pictures I had to redirect my focus.

At first, the Idealizing of my childhood was dominant, then after a few days, I didn't have to Idealize my childhood as much and I could focus on my job, my weight and my relationship Ideals. Anytime during my day, if the old feelings of unworthiness came back, I would Idealize my perfect childhood again. It was almost like replaying my favorite movie over and over in my mind.

After just days, I lost my craving for junk food. I craved vegetables and fruit instead. I have created some of the best tasting salads. I lost weight without working at it. I Idealized my perfect weight and was then motivated to stat taking the stairs instead of the elevator; or parking at the end of the parking lot and walking the distance instead of driving around looking for the closest space with the shortest walk. After about 2 weeks of Idealizing, I got an unexpected promotion and raise at work. The extra income was just what I was Idealizing would take care of my current bills. I am Idealizing myself working at my new position and being proud of myself. My relationships with my friends is improving, and just today, a handsome man flirted with me at the grocery store. That was great. I deserved it. ☺

I am still seeing changes in my life, and adding and changing my Ideals. Every day, as I feel more worthy, I can see more of what I deserve and I expand my Ideals.

I still Idealize my childhood anytime those old feelings come up, but they are much less.

Until I got to the old damaging messages that were rooted in me, I couldn't understand how I could make changes in my life. Getting specific on my desires so I could Idealize them was a lot or work at the start, but I'm worth it. Now I see more possibilities". .~ SPB, Orange, CA,~ Name Withheld by Request,

Chapter 10

GIVING A BODY OF ETHERIC SUBSTANCE TO YOUR IDEAL

The next step is to create a body for your *Ideal*, a body of real etheric substance. Image the *Ideal* of the thing you want. Does the thing itself seem so compact and dense that you cannot re-form and re-create it to accord with your *Ideal*? Its form can be changed, but only if you give a body to your *Ideal*.

First, give form to the substance of the *Ideal*. Turn back and read again my third Chapter. Then, re-*Idealize* your image of the thing desired as made of infinite energy-space. By doing this you actually group the spiritual substance into form. This is a first step in creating the body of your *Ideal*.

Second, give the body attractive power. Read again the fourth Chapter of this book. Then, re-image your *Ideal* of the thing you want. Realize, that whatever the substance of the thing desired, that which makes its actuality possible is infinite attractive energy; that it is this same energy that holds all the particles of your *Ideal* together and draws to it all the factors necessary for manifestation. By thus imaging your *Ideal* you give it solidity. The particles of this spiritual substance become fixed so that the *Ideal* will persist; so that it will not change, as an idea changes, or evaporate in vain imaging's. By this process you also give it power to attract and draw to it all those conditions, qualities, thoughts, feelings and attitudes necessary to make it real, necessary to make its actuality possible.

Third, create the body of self-active substance. Turn back and read the fifth Chapter. Realize that everything you wish to change is in infinite motion, thrilling with life;

that even the piece of copper wire that leads to your electric light is composed of whirling centers of space, infinitely small, capable of moving 660,000,000 miles an hour and able to change their positions 40,000,000 times a second, By this process you rid your soul of any idea that any so-called material thing can oppose the manifestation of your *Ideal*. And you give to the *Ideal*, to its body substance, the same quality of infinite, infinitely rapid power of movement, power of action, power to make itself come true.

Imagine the body of your *Ideal* composed of spirit substance, vibrating at this tremendous rate, exerting enormous power, and you give it additional power to make itself into an actuality. To this point in the process, what is your *Ideal*?

First, a perfect image, including only those elements it should possess and none that it should not possess.

Second, an *Ideal* with a heart of desire, fired to action by all your feelings and soul desires: (1) increased by imaging the beauty and utility of the *Ideal* and the pleasures it will give you and (2) augmented by every conceivable element of desire you can awaken by imaging everything composing its image, color, sound, and etcetera.

Third, an *Ideal* body, formed of the infinite spirit substance, energy-ether; a body of the same material as the essence of matter which makes it easy for the *Ideal* to manifest as an actuality; a body held together and made permanent by infinite attractive energy; a body composed of etheric substance whose particles vibrate at a rate so rapid that imagination cannot conceive it; a body composed of etheric substance an ounce of which has gigantic power, sufficient if freed at one time, to toss the Alps into the Atlantic Ocean.

Now give the *Ideal* the soul impulse to act, and you cannot prevent its coming true.

"When your desires are strong enough, you will appear to possess superhuman powers to achieve."

~ Napoleon Hill ~

CHAPTER 11

GIVING YOUR IDEAL THE IMPULSE OF ACTION TO MAKE IT REAL

There is one more step in the process of making your *Ideal* complete. It possesses infinite energy, but you must give it the impulse of action. How can you do this? In this I differ from many others. I hold that visualization is not sufficient. Visualization, although it often accomplishes wonders, is after all but a picturing of an idea. It does make the idea vivid but it adds to it only one of several elements, only the images of the sight sense.

Instead of visualization I use *Idealization*, **the perfect image.** This includes the factor of visualization and that of the eleven other factors. Using the other factors, especially those of motion and direction of motion, we give the *Ideal* an impulse to move and this in turn gives it the action power that makes the *Ideal* manifest as a reality.

Visualizing is the act of holding a mental picture; *Idealizing* is the act of perfecting the mental image of all factors, the picture, the process of securing it and the act of making it real.

You often ignite the heart of your *Ideal* by vivid mental pictures and strong feelings of desire to possess the reality; but unless connected up with your motor power of action, it remains merely an urgent unfulfilled picture of desire within you, an *Ideal* that does not become a reality. Clutching your *Ideal* to action cannot be effectively accomplished by a picture. Let me illustrate this clearly.

Go to an art museum; look at any painting representing a number of people. If, after going away, you close your eyes and visualize the painting, you hold in your mind a mental picture of the painting. With care and practice you can make this mental picture very vivid and increase your ability to re-see in the mind every detail of such a painting, lines, forms and colors of things and people. Yet, it is still a mere picture; it is flat, lacking action, and it does not impel to action. That which I have just described is the visualizing process. Visualizing has produced marvelous results when the person visualizing has turned such mental picture-making into the *Idealized* process, even if they have not recognized that they have done so.

Idealizing, however, is more remarkable because it includes visualizing and adds all other elements to it. Visualization comes from using the stored-up images of but one of our senses, the sense of sight. *Idealization* comes from using the stored-up images not only of the sense of sight but of all other senses. To attain that which we desire it is necessary, not only to see the visual image, but to act.

Try now another process: *Idealize* the painting you saw in the art museum; bring it visually to your mind; re-see it just as you did by the process previously described. Then image action, every person in it in action; feel them doing the thing they are pictured as doing; feel the movement; feel the activities. If it portrays them as speaking, hear the tones, hear what they say. I might continue with all other elements of the picture, but I think this is sufficient to show you the difference between visualization and *Idealization* . Visualization produces a nonmoving, non-active picture in the mind, even though it be vivid and clear. Being non-active, it does not impel to action and hence many of our pictured *Ideals* do not become realities. But if we *Idealize* action, if we use the mental clutch of connecting up the *Ideal* of the thing desired with the process of obtaining that which we desire, action must result; and action is one of the essential factors in making any *Ideal* come true.

"*Nothing is forgotten in the processes of*

Idealization."

~ Gaston Bachelard ~

CHAPTER 12

THE PROCESS THAT MAKES IDEALS COME TRUE

Process is the way of doing things. There are several ways of doing things, but the *Idealized* way is the only way that guarantees success.

The non-*Idealized* processes are: mere doing; purposeful doing; planned or thought-out doing.

The fourth process is the *Idealized* process.

Mere doing never leads to success, for back of it there is no *Ideal* of the process, no desire to improve it, no thought-out plan, and no *Ideal*. In mines and stores and factories and offices, there are millions of good workers. They learn to do one thing, they learn to do it well, and then, forever afterwards, they merely do. They drudge, or toil, or labor but they do not work; and, they do not succeed.

You yourself may do your work perfectly merely doing it; you may be always at it; others may be able to depend upon you doing your work exactly, with no loss of time, not missing a stroke. But all these do not lead to attainment, why, even a hay-press does those things!

Purposeful doing is one step in advance of mere doing. It is based upon an idea of progress and is stimulated by a desire. But that is not sufficient. Why, the bank-robber has a purpose in robbing; he may succeed now and then in getting what he wants and he always succeeds in making himself a useless member of society; yet, his life is not successful and he is not a success. Even well planned, carefully thought-out doing leads to thousands of failures. Many a young man,

95

intelligent, enthusiastic, hardworking and earnest, starts in business for himself and fails, even after he has planned and thought out his entire problem. When he begins, he sees success, big success, within two or three years at most. But in six months the sheriff may close him up as a failure. Even planned doing, based upon ideas, desires and thought-out processes, fails *unless the process is Idealized*. It is only an *Idealized* aim, process and attitude that always win.

Some time ago an additional main subway was opened in New York City. It necessitated a new routing of passengers. More than seven million people had to learn to travel by new routes. For days before its opening the papers were full of the new system and how to get from one point to another. At least nine out of every ten of the millions of adults in New York must have read the directions previous to the opening, although probably not one in a hundred thousand, when they read the directions over and over again, *Idealized* the new route, nor *Idealized* themselves going about the city or to and from work on it. The Result of Not *Idealizing* the

Process on the day of the opening, intelligent men and women crowded and jammed each other, went where they did not wish to go, even got lost, though many of them had known New York all their lives. The confusion and jamming of the mob at two transfer stations were so great that scores of women fainted, and many were seriously hurt. More than a million people lost their heads; more than a million were confused for weeks. It was necessary to close the cross-town subway for a month to prevent accidents -actually to prevent people killing themselves and each other, because of their confused mob action. And all of this confusion, trouble, injury and delay could have been prevented if each of the seven million people who use the subways had spent but five minutes previous to its opening in *Idealizing* the Process of traveling on it.

How I *Idealized* the Process in this Case: I took a description of the routes from a newspaper; read it carefully. Then I quietly visualized the new routes. Next, I *Idealized* action, *Idealized* myself using the new route from my home to my office, picturing myself on the cars, changing where the description said changes must be made; *Idealizing* every bit of the journey to my office door. Next I *Idealized* one trip after another to other parts of the city, until I had myself mentally used every new and old route. After this, it was impossible to be confused; impossible to make a mistake in using the subway.

Millions of others thought of the new routes, but certainly very few consciously *Idealized* themselves traveling on them. Yet every individual in New York could have done it in five minutes if they had only been in the habit of *Idealizing* the Process of Doing Things. Others had ideas of the new route, of where they wanted to go, and of how to get there. I turned my ideas into *Ideals*. *Idealizing* the process of doing the thing, included more than the re-seeing of the mental picture of the new route. I did more than visualize it. I put into it an element of action. I kept my "clutch" in so that the picture became movement. That is always essential in attaining that which you desire.

"There is one who gets any further than warming the
teapot. He's a rare fine hand at that.
Feel this teapot. Is it not beautifully warm?
Yes, but there ain't going to be no tea."
~ Katherine Mansfield ~

CHAPTER 13

THE ACT OF MAKING THE REALITY YOURS

This last activity, the act of making the reality yours, comprises three steps:

(1) *Idealizing* your attitude;

(2) unifying the substance of the *Ideal* WITH the substance of the real; and

(3) making the actual thing a part of your possessions or placing yourself in the actual conditions that you have *Idealized* and desired.

Your attitude relates to yourself, to others, to conditions, and to the world in general. Begin with yourself. Consciously or not, you do take some kind of an attitude toward yourself. You may think yourself a worm or a Divine Spiritual Source. You are free to take any attitude toward yourself you desire to take; but there is only one attitude that leads to success and it is the *Idealized* attitude! Incomplete thinking in "ideas" makes you see yourself as a child of sin, suffering, sorrow, weakness, mistake and failure. Think of yourself as you are: a son of Divine Spiritual Source, *Idealizing* the end you desire, the process by which you attain, and the attitude you hold toward yourself, others, conditions, and the universe itself.

Then, *Idealize* your attitude toward others, "That which ye seek ye shall find." If you think that all men are trying to crush you, you will be crushed; first, because your attitude closes your eyes to the opportunities offered you; and second, because such an attitude discovers and draws to you those who do not help you. If you *Idealize* others as willing to help you, you draw to you men and women who will do the square thing by you and help you; in them you will find help and a just reward. This *Idealized* attitude does not make you a trusting simpleton, for the *Idealized* attitude also *Idealize*s wisdom in knowing others.

The *Idealized* attitude changes all the conditions of life. In business, it leads us to expect good results, and, expecting good results, we plan better. When we plan better, that is, in, a more *Idealized* way, we get better results. *Idealize* the world in general. The universe must be good. If it were not good it would go to pieces over night, for evil disrupts and destroys. Good attracts and unites and holds together.

You cannot *Idealize* your business, your profession and your work without conducting the whole affair as an *Idealized* service that inevitably will force your *Ideals* to come true! You may *Idealize* the Thing Desired, *Idealize* the Process of Attaining It and Carry Out the Process in Action, and, yet, by your attitude keep the reality from becoming yours. With a group of congenial friends, you can desire and *Idealize* an evening's pleasure for yourself and the girl you love, you may call for her and go to the gathering together, and yet your attitude, if disagreeable, can keep the pleasure of the evening from becoming yours.

First, then, give attention to your attitude! Second, unify the substance of your *Ideal* with the substance of the thing or condition desired. The substance of your *Ideal* is yours! It is of your mind. The substance of the reality may not yet be yours. To make it yours, you must make the body of your *Ideal* coincide with the body or actuality of that which you desire.

Re-read the Chapters on How to Form an *Ideal* that Will Come True, Firing the Heart Desire of Your *Ideal*, Giving a Body of Etheric Substance to Your *Ideal*, and Giving Your *Ideal* the Impulse of Action to Make It Real. Then, re-image your *Ideal* in accord with those four qualities; its form, its desire, its substance, its impulse to action.

Next, re-read the three Chapters of The Spirit of Matter: Your *Ideals* and What Compactness of Matter Gives to Them, Your Desires and What Attractive Energy Gives to Them, What Movement in Matter Gives to the Body of Your Desire. Do not neglect to re-read these. You remember much, but not all the things.

Re-read them, recognizing:

(a) that the material density, of the thing you desire is an etheric substance coinciding in nature with the substance of your *Ideal*;

(b) that the material solidity of the thing you desire is infinite attractive energy which coincides in nature with the holding-together energy of your *Ideal*; and

(c) that the energy of the material thing desired is etheric force -exactly the same force as exists in your *Ideal*.

Now, image each detail of your *Ideal*, project it out of your mind to the place of the actuality, and unite it with the same detail of the material actuality you desire to be yours. Do not miss a single detail; make the projected *Ideal* coincide with the actual thing in every feature - form, substance, energy and place. To miss no factor, unify step by step, as to color, sound, taste, smell, balance, heat, movement, direction of movement, form, size, fineness or roughness, hardness or softness, cold, weight, use, pleasures from use, et cetera. Miss none of these!

Then, third, take possession of the thing or walk into the condition desired. *Idealize* yourself in action:

(1) the condition of yourself when in action; and

(2) your use of the means to be used in performing your action.

If this afternoon you are to go to one man or a group of men to discuss or do something which it is necessary for you to present or do in order to make your *Ideal* come true, image yourself with the man or with the men, image yourself at perfect ease, image your confidence in yourself, image your self-control when talking to them, when contradicted by them, even when ridiculed by one or more of them. Image these conditions in your mind before you go. It builds in brain a path that makes the doing of the thing but a mere repetition of a thing already done.

I say image these things, not merely imagine them; merely thinking about them will not bring results. Image also the impressions you see yourself giving to others: Are you appearing as sincere as you are sincere! Are you appearing as reliable as you are reliable? Are you appearing active and energetic and sane and safe? Remember, it is not only what you are, but what you communicate to others which determine results in dealing with others.

Idealizing the action builds-in brain paths. Then, when you come to the actual doing, you have already established a habit of doing it successfully. The more times you *Idealize* the doing, the stronger and more permanent these brain paths become. Hence, when you go into action, you are merely repeating what you have already done and what you have already succeeded in doing. Consequently there is no hesitancy, no doubt, no lack of confidence, no lack of ease, and no mistakes in your action. And, because you center your effort rightly the thing or condition is a reality and belongs to you!

Where to center your effort now follows.

"The trick is in what one emphasizes.
We either make ourselves miserable,
or we make ourselves happy.
The amount of work is the same."
~ Carlos Castaneda ~

CHAPTER 14

WHERE TO CENTER YOUR EFFORT

It is very important that you *Idealize* that which you desire; but, so far as the attainment of it is concerned, the process is much more important, and *Idealizing* the process is the most important of all. I will illustrate (1) by a little incident and (2) by a great world experience.

In the spring of 1919, sometime after I had returned to the United States from one of my sojourns abroad, I wrote a letter to Elizabeth Towne. I had known her for many years but while I was living abroad we had been quite out of touch. When Mrs. Towne received my letter it awakened a desire in her mind. There was to be a convention near her hometown the following week. She wished me to speak at that convention. To have me speak at the convention was her *Ideal* of the Thing Desired. Did she stop with the *Ideal* of the thing desired? Not at all. She began *Idealizing* the Process of getting me there. She pressed the bell-button immediately; in came a stenographer; and a letter was sent telling me how I could come and return, giving information of the trains, how, by traveling at night, the trip would take the least possible time. At intervals during that day and next she went on *Idealizing* the Process of arranging for me while there, where I should stay, when I should speak, how many times I should speak, et cetera, et cetera. **She gave ten seconds to recognizing the *Ideal* of the Thing Desired and an hour or more *Idealizing* the Process:** 10 seconds to the former; 3,600 seconds to the latter. That's about the right proportion.

Think this over; it applies to everything in life. Give about a thousand times more time and effort to *Idealizing* and working out the process than you give to *Idealizing* the thing you desire and your *Ideal* will come true. Turn from this very simple incident to consider the value of *Idealizing* the Process in attaining great things, any very great thing, in such a matter as a world war.

The great World War was a great spiritual test of the race. When the Germans in 1914 were at the Marne, the *Ideal* of the Thing Desired was: the German Army must be stopped! This was not a mere idea; it was a life and death *Ideal* of the peoples of the Allied countries. Great leaders recognized this. When news that the German Army was being forced back was ticked off in the London War Office, Lord Kitchener said, "must have done it"; and Lord Roberts replied, "It means the nations have been praying." The following year, during another crisis, Lloyd George exclaimed, "The war will be lost unless all England gets down on her knees in prayer;" and in 1918 the great Foch found daily communion necessary. This was the emphasis of the *Ideal*.

But the Process was not neglected. Even he, who daily spent an hour in prayer and daily went to Holy Communion, knew that Divine Spiritual Source helps only those who know enough to help themselves. Our one national war-*Ideal* was: Win! Having once recognized this, did we waste time harping upon it? No! And we succeeded because we centered most of our efforts upon the processes necessary to win the war. When it was necessary to save food we saved it. We went without this or that, without meat on meatless days; without wheat on wheatless days. But we did more than accept the process; we *Idealized* it. We made it a matter of patriotism; a religion of brotherly help to our allies who needed food.

When, we needed money, did we continue harping on the *Ideal*? Not at all! We *Idealized* the Process of furnishing the means to equip and feed our boys. We *Idealized* the Process to such an extent that he who did not buy all he could afford and a little more, felt wrong inside. When more ships were needed college boys and highly paid business men did manual work in the ship yards; and when more munitions were needed, women whose white hands had never before known the grease of factory machines, worked long hours because the process was *Idealized*.

111

What was new in this: we had always held *Ideals* and been forced to take part in the processes of life in peace times. The new thing, the thing that brought phenomenal results, was the *Idealization* of the Process. No work was drudgery; it was an *Idealized* Part of the Efforts of a Great Human Brotherhood. Suppose we had neglected the Process! Suppose we had made no munitions, built no ships, sold no bonds, sent no men oversea, would such procedure have helped to win the war?! Such a process would have been ridiculous. Yet, in other matters, we attempt to make our *Ideals* and desires come true by holding persistently day after day and month after month to the *Ideal* of the Thing Desired, giving little or no attention to *Idealizing* the process and putting it into operation.

If you want to win, if you really wish that which you desire, if you truly desire to make your *Ideals* come true, to turn them into realities, first form your *Ideal* of the Thing Desired but give your great effort to *Idealizing* the Process and putting it into action. That brings you the reality!

"I prayed for twenty years but received no answer

until I prayed with my legs."

~ Frederick Douglass ~

IDEALIZING THINGS

CHAPTER 15

IDEALIZED THINGS MAKE FORTUNES

In whatever you are doing and in whatever you hope to do and attain, it is necessary to deal with three factors: things, words and people. In fact, when you come to think of it, there is nothing else with which you can deal. Consequently, *Idealizing* the process of attaining what you want includes *Idealizing* the things with which you work or the things you are to handle; and often great fortunes are made from *Idealizing* little things and great failures result from non-*Idealization* of things, big or little. Here are the experiences of two men illustrating the point.

It was on the train speeding across the State of New York toward Chicago. I had left the dining car, gone to the Club car and, observing that the seats about one of the card tables were empty, sat down there so that I might be alone to read. Men were coming in from dinner and soon a man took a seat across the table. I looked up to determine whether others were with him and, if so, whether they might not wish the table for card playing. But he was alone. He had a fine face, clean, clear-cut; evidently a man of education; perhaps, a man of culture. His face, his bearing, his attitude all proclaimed him to be a "man of *Ideals*." I do not mean a visionary, but a man who does and who has always done that which is right and who refuses and has refused to do that which is wrong.

In a minute we were in conversation. It started regarding the high cost of living. It went from one thing to another. He was communicative and it was not long before he mentioned that he had wished this year to send his boy to college but he had been unable to do so because he could not afford it. "A college education costs four times as much today as it did when I went to college," he said.

The first point I wish you to remember is this: he could not afford to send his son to college. I led him on in the conversation, learned that after graduating from college he had been a school teacher; that later he had been in Y. M. C. A. work; a welfare worker in a manufacturing plant for a year; and that in 1913, he, with a friend, had gone into a manufacturing business of his own. "What line of manufacturing? " I asked. "Oh, just little wicker hand satchels, such as boys use to carry books to and from school," he answered. This is the second point I wish you to remember: "Oh, just little wicker hand satchels." This conversation took place in the year 1920. It indicates that after having been in business seven years, manufacturing an article of use to at least ten million school children as well as hundreds of thousands of others in our country, this "man of *Ideals*" was unable to send his boy to college because he could not afford it. We talked of other things; but before long he left me, going back to his private car. Two other men came in and sat down. One across the table, one beside me. Later I learned that one was a coal operator of Indiana, and the other, -well, the rest of the story concerns the other man.

One look at this man told me he was not a so-called "man of *Ideals*," -that is, not in accord with the ordinary use of the term. He looked very prosperous; he was talkative -men are always more communicative after dinner, smoking a good cigar, on a train with nothing else to do. This man is the soap-dye king of the world. Only a few years ago he and a friend, his wife and his friend's wife, started in business making soap-dyes. Altogether they had $800. Today each of them is more than a millionaire. Their soap-dyes sell for ten cents a package, yet they do a business of many hundred thousand dollars a month. They secured the original patent and consequently, in addition to the profits they make from their own concern, they are paid royalties by all other soap-dye companies.

How did he do it? I have said that he is not a man of *Ideals*. That statement is both true and not true. He is not a man of *Ideals* of the Pharisee kind, but he is a man who *Idealize*s the thing with which he works. To him the soap-dye is one of the great inventions of the age. His face glowed as he told about it; his eyes shone.

"Think what it means," he said, "for every woman in the land -in fact, all over the world, for now we're selling soap-dyes to Europe, Australia, India and Japan -to be able in two minutes to change the color of her shirtwaist, of a piece of lace, or any light trimming merely by dipping it in our dye, without any boiling, and without staining her hands."

From the very beginning he had *Idealized* the thing he produced. He had *Idealized* the soap in order to select the best for the purpose. He had *Idealized* the dyes so as to produce the most useful dye; the most easily and quickly used dye; a dye needing no boiling; a dye that does not stain the hands of those using it. He had *Idealized* the chemicals used in the process of making the dye, and, as he talked of how he had built up the business, I saw that he had even *Idealized* the kind of chemical expert he wanted and had then searched the United States until he found the man that fitted his *Ideal*. He had *Idealized* justice and had secured patent rights for himself and those who had worked for him.

His process of *Idealizing* the thing -the soap-dye -did not stop when he had put a good product on the market and when that product had earned him millions of dollars. He told me how that very afternoon he had spent three hours with Japanese young women in New York to prove his soap-dyes would not stain the hands of the Japanese women. He had done this because reports had come from Japan that the dyes did stain the hands of Japanese young women.

He began his work by *Idealizing* the thing he intended to manufacture; he had *Idealized* the thing every day since he first conceived it; and he is still *Idealizing* that same thing. Is it any wonder that his face glows, that his eyes shine, that his tone is enthusiastic and that he is making millions? He is not a so-called "man of *Ideals*," but he puts *Idealizing* into action. He *Idealize*s everything, even common labor; he was actually happy telling me that he and his wife made the first dyes in their own home in stew pots and dish-pans and that, while he was making the boxes in which to ship the dyes, his wife was out peddling them. He has *Idealized* the service the dyes render to millions of women and the just rewards to himself. Consequently, he is successful. He is worth millions, made in less than four years; he was able to send his two boys to college.

There are Pharisees today as there were in Christ's time. What value are your *Ideals* unless you use them? The great master has said that unless we use the talents we have even that which we have shall be taken away. It is not holding *Ideals* that make desires come true. It is using *Ideals*. The first step is to *Idealize* the thing with which you are working.

CHAPTER 16

A BILLION DOLLARS BY IDEALIZING THE MOVEMENT OF THINGS

Everyone wants abundance, abundance of all things! And, specifically, everyone wants money and all things that take the place of money. Can you turn a desire for money directly into money? No, certainly not! Money is the result of abundance, not abundance itself. Let us agree upon the meaning of the term. When one friend is thinking of a Persian cat and another is thinking of an ordinary house cat, both will disagree with what I am saying about a cat if I am thinking and talking of a wild cat. Therefore qualify at once the word abundance. One meaning of the word is sufficiency -enough to meet all our true needs, present and future.

Idealizing the Process to Secure Abundance should not be limited to securing money directly. Other factors are more important. They are an abundance of ideas, recognition of the abundant opportunities that surround you, and being abundantly prepared to make use of them. Lack of material abundance is not a lack of ideas; but money-lack always indicates a poverty of *Ideals* regarding the right processes of getting money.

Once all hairpins were made of straight wire and were always moving, always slipping out of the lady's hair. Millions of women were disturbed about it for scores of years and many people, millions of them, had ideas about it. Hundreds of thousands consciously desired and wished for something better and thought about it. Nothing, however, resulted from the ideas and thoughts of these hundreds of thousands. Not a one of them ever made a cent out of his or her ideas or thoughts. There was no abundance in them. But, there was abundance in the *Ideal* of a hairpin which of itself prevented itself from moving easily. The man who *Idealized* and produced the crinkly wire hairpin is now a multi-millionaire.

Abundance always resides in an *Ideal*, whether of property or management or manufacturing or position or what not; it resides in *Idealizing* even the detailed parts of things and the movement of so common a substance as oil. The steps in the *Idealizing* Process which brought success to Mr. Rockefeller were: First, he *Idealized* oil in detail. The other oilmen, then wealthier than Mr. Rockefeller, thought of oil only as oil; as costing so much per barrel, as selling for so much, and as bringing so much profit.

Mr. Rockefeller thought of these things, but in addition he *Idealized* oil in all its details. Mentally he visioned other substances in it, not at all like oil. Moreover, he *Idealized* the processes of separating these from the oil, and out of these came the by-products. Today, it is said, the Standard Oil Company could give away all its oil and yet pay good dividends out of the profits of its by-products. Let us be just: this wealth from the byproducts was due to the fact that Mr. Rockefeller was less realistic than others; he *Idealized* the oil that to others was just oil and nothing more.

Second, Mr. Rockefeller *Idealized* the movement of oil. Other oilmen thought of transporting oil just as barrels of flour and barrels of sugar are transported. But Mr. Rockefeller *Idealized* it in motion; he saw it flowing and *Idealized* it flowing in pipes. Hence the pipeline system, the second great source of Standard Oil profits and supremacy. Again let us be just Divine Spiritual Source, and His laws rule: Mr. Rockefeller won phenomenal financial success because he *Idealized*, more than did his competitors, the detailed parts of the thing and its movement.

On the other hand, Mr. Rockefeller did not *Idealize* his relation to the rest of society. He thought of himself as a man standing alone. For forty years he was silent, unwilling that anyone within his companies should give any statement regarding their policies or methods to the public. He failed to *Idealize* the truth that men are bound together in a social structure and consequently, separating himself from others, he failed to win the trust and good will of mankind. Ideas, thoughts composed of ideas, and plans made up of such thoughts seldom become realities. But once the smallest or the largest thing is *Idealized*, the soul, which conceives the *Ideal*, cannot rest until the *Ideal* has become an actuality. If you would have your desires for abundance fulfilled, *Idealize* them and the process of obtaining them, and abundance cannot be kept from you.

IDEALIZING
MEANS
AND METHODS

CHAPTER 17

BUILDING UP A SUCCESSFUL BUSINESS

In business you fail in some things and succeed in others. You are often failing and succeeding at the same time, failing to make one part of your business successful and succeeding in making another part increase and pay. The failures are due to the ideas held; the successes, to the *Ideals*. If you *Idealize* the entire process of your business you will not only avoid failures and partial failures, but will think of possibilities never thought of before, the very ones that will lead you to succeed. To illustrate, I shall use a simple case, one of the simplest that ever came to me, yet one of the most interesting, and one, the success of which, gave me as much joy as the success of many so-called big affairs. In this instance there was a woman in the case, and it's her story I shall tell.

The Woman: A widow with four children; she then lived in a suburb of Chicago; her husband had died three months before; she was left as proprietor of a small grocery and delicatessen store.

The Conditions: As the husband had been ill three months before his death, savings had been used in doctor bills, hospital bills and funeral expenses. Though the store was a little affair, it had had a good business in this section of the wealthy suburb so long as it had been the only store there. But, about the time of the husband's death, one of those large companies that establish branch stores all over a great city built a white-tiled, plate-glass, two-story building on the corner opposite her little shop. It cut down the business of the little store so much that the woman was unable even to make a living for herself and her children.

The Problem: I confess when she first told me the entire story that it seemed impossible for her to compete with the new store with all its service, its supplies, and its million-dollar parent company back of it.

The First Step: The first thought was: Divine Spiritual Source, is not only All Supply, but He is also All Process and Means; the second, Since Divine Spiritual Source, is All Process and Means, He knows and has all ideas necessary to make this store a success; and the third, Since Divine Spiritual Source's ideas are *Ideal*, we can get in touch with them as soon as we *Idealize* our own.

How We Went About It: We *Idealized*

(1) those to whom she could sell,

(2) the business itself, and

(3) the woman.

Visualizing the people of the community was a simple matter. All were medium well-to-do; most families had two or more maids; they entertained often at their homes, dinner parties and evening affairs. But what could this woman sell to them which the other store could not supply?

Idealizing the Business: The woman told me the greatest profit was made in handling bakery goods. The big bakeries of the city delivered goods each morning and took back what was left unsold of the day before. In this line there was no waste, and no loss. Moreover, the profit on the amount invested was made daily. If the woman invested ten dollars in canned goods, it might be a month before all were sold; if she made a ten percent profit she made but ten percent on ten dollars in a month. But with bakery goods, if she invested ten dollars in the morning and sold the goods during the day at ten percent profit, she made ten percent on ten dollars in one day.

Evidently in this case bakery goods was to be the leader; but how could this little woman make her bakery goods lead over the goods of the other store, when both of them could buy from the same bakeries; and the other store had more money than she, and hence could buy better and more extensive supplies than she could?

Idealizing the Woman: All the time she talked, I had a feeling of conflicting ideas in my mind about her. These remained indefinite until it flashed upon me that, although her name was Mrs. Hansen (Scandinavian), she spoke with a Scotch accent.

The New Thought: Scotch, Scotland, Scotch tarts, those delicious uncovered fruit pies, two-and-a-half and three inches deep, and as big as a dinner plate, Scotch tarts, which only Scotch and English women know how to make. "Are you Scotch?" I asked. " Yes," she replied, evidently surprised. "Can you make Scotch tarts?" "Yes; at least I used to." "Then go down in my kitchen and make one; order anything you think necessary, but make the best one you know how to make." That night I tasted a tart equal to any I had ever eaten; and the next morning she started the pie industry. I sent a note out to a few acquaintances, telling them the old pagan Divine Spiritual Source, on Mount Olympus would still be contentedly happy, even if nectar were taken from them, providing they could get real Scotch tarts; also that I had found a Scotch woman who could make just such tarts, and that these delicious desserts could be secured in Chicago; and I also added that they'd be wise to send their maids early in the morning with an order to Mrs. Hansen.

The Success: The first day she made a dozen pies and sold every one of them. At a good price, too, for these were no dollar pies. These pies were pies, apple tart three inches deep, with gooseberry sauce to be served with whipped cream. They were worth much as pies, but much more as distinctive desserts not procurable elsewhere. Of course the pie business grew and grew. Moreover, as families bought their tarts from Mrs. Hansen, their maids also ordered other things at the same time. The *Idealized* leader became the actual leader of group after group of other goods sold from the shelves of her store.

Idealizing the Process: Divine Spiritual Source, working in every step led us to get the New Idea, the new thought of making Scotch tarts. Common sense? Yes. Only common sense? No. It was _Idealized_ Common Sense. Divine Spiritual Source is all Process, and Divine Spiritual Source Ideas are your ideas, unlimited, as soon as you _Idealize_ your own thought processes so as to be in touch with Divine Spiritual Source.

"Our duty, as men and women, is to proceed as if

limits to our ability did not exist.

We are collaborators in creation. "

~ Pierre Teilhard de Chardin ~

CHAPTER 18

FIVE MINUTES IDEALIZING A DAY MAKES YOU SUPER-EFFICIENT

Someone once said, "Order is Heaven's first Law." Who it was I do not know. It was first said thousands of years ago and I am not old enough to remember. But the saying being old and persisting through the ages, I know it must be very true else the race would not have conceived it and kept it alive in our consciousness. Heaven is the Kingdom of Divine Spiritual Source. Order is Divine Spiritual Source's first Law. Without order in the process of your thinking and order in the act of doing things, *Ideals* and desires do not come true. The value of

Idealizing a series of things to be done before starting to do them is well illustrated by this experience:

The Scene: Office of a physician in a South American city. City just visited by cyclone; destruction freaky as to places; some telephone exchanges in order; houses here and there almost completely destroyed; many others not damaged; yet scores of people severely injured by falling walls.

The Work to be Done: As the cyclone passed, many telephone messages begged the physician's immediate assistance. The first asked him to hurry to a certain place to attend a woman whose scalp was torn and who evidently was suffering from internal injuries, and he was about to leave when the second message from another place begged him to come there at once and attend a man with a broken leg and an injured back. Message followed message, two score and more, each of which he listed. It was then he changed his plans; and even though he realized that each case should be attended quickly, he did not rush off.

The First Thing He Did: He took the receiver from his telephone, for there was no need of listing more calls; these and those he would find would be all he could attend to. Then for five minutes he sat quietly at his desk, seemingly doing nothing.

The Second Thing: Quickly he wrote a list of medicines, cottons, bandages, etc., and calling his office girl, told her to rush to the druggist at the corner, to insist they be given her at once, and to wait with them outside the druggist's door till he came.

The Third Thing: He telephoned the department store a block beyond the drug store and ordered a clerk to stand ready with fifty blankets at the door of the store.

The Fourth Thing: He rapidly selected from his operating room every instrument that might be necessary in any kind of emergency case.

The Fifth Thing: Taking his bags of instruments and his medicine cases, he ran to his auto at the door; drove to the drug store corner, where, without stopping his machine, he snatched the package from the girl; and continued on to the department store, where he commanded the clerk to dump the blankets in the car.

The Sixth Thing: Then, and only then, did he begin his work of assistance, going rapidly from one injured person to another.

The Result: In no case was anything lacking that was needed; and the records show that during the afternoon he attended twice as many injured as any other physician of the city. The result of his work shows that his efforts of the afternoon were most efficient. But what did he do while sitting at his desk? Did he waste those first five minutes? This is what he did:

First, he *Idealized* all the different kinds of injuries reported to him, and, in addition, all the possible injuries he might be called upon to treat;

Second, he visualized all of the medicines, antiseptics, accessories, etc., that would be required and might be required; visioned his own supply and such a surplus to be obtained at the drug store as would make any lack impossible;

Third, he *Idealized* what should be done at once to aid the future recovery of those injured, the wisdom of wrapping each up in a warm blanket immediately after the first aid, as protection from the after-chill of the storm;

Fourth, he visualized the places where the most seriously injured were reported to be; *Idealized* Itself going from one to another by shortest routes; and repeated the process, visioning the places where the less seriously injured were. All this in five minutes!

Yes, the mind, trained to *Idealize* the Process and knowing that Divine Spiritual Source, is in every process, works more rapidly than radio.

Were the first five minutes wasted? Those five minutes more than doubled his service that afternoon and evening, and there was no failure to give aid because some necessary thing was lacking. But we, yes, we see the value of *Idealizing* the Process of Doing Things in an emergency; but we forget that in our lives each hour is an emergency, a call to do the most, live the most.

"What you are will show in what you do. "

~ Thomas A. Edison ~

CHAPTER 19

TURNING DESIRES FOR SALES INTO ACTUAL SALES

In essence every phase of contact in human society is a sale. If you apply for and secure a position you sell yourself to the employer, who buys your services in competition with many others. If you are the leader of a great reform movement, carrying the *Ideal* of that reform to the masses of people and winning them to support it, you are selling your *Ideals* to them. Of course there are business sales, for every phase of business operation and management is a sale of things, ideas, and *Ideals* of services. The process of selling is always the same. Any sale you desire to make, any sale you have in mind as an *Ideal*, can be made a reality; but every "idea" you have of a sale may fall through.

If you *Idealize* the value of that which you wish to sell, you give it additional selling value. If you *Idealize* the process of selling it, you discover new means of selling. If you *Idealize* all kinds of possible buyers of that which you have for sale, you discover a buyer capable of perceiving the additional value you have given your product and a buyer capable and willing to pay for that value.

A Case for Illustration: A man owned a tract of land near Pasadena, California; on this there was a $10,000 mortgage; he had bought it on a shoestring, planning soon to sell it, for it was expected that a building boom would make it a desirable residence site long before the $10,000 was due.

Conditions at End of Six Months: The building boom had not materialized; the mortgage was due in ten days; real estate men refused to take it up; those holding the mortgage refused to extend it; the bankers wouldn't touch it.

Cause for Refusal: The land was in a hollow; real estate men and bankers were convinced no one would buy it until every other residence site near it had been sold; that might be years hence.

The Owner's First Efforts: When, at the end of the first three months, the boom failed to boom, he recognized abundant supply, and faithfully and persistently and confidently affirmed "Divine Spiritual Source, IS ALL Abundance" and "All is Divine Spiritual Source."

Three months went by. The money did not drop from the heaven; but something else dropped, the corners of his banker's mouth. What was the trouble? Faithfully and confidently the owner affirmed the truth: "Divine Spiritual Source Is the Source of Abundant Supply." Why then the failure? Because Divine Spiritual Source, is Spirit; and consequently as long as he continued merely to affirm Divine Spiritual Source, as Abundant Supply, the supply continued in a spiritual state. This the bankers refused to cash; they wanted certified checks. After a failure of more than two and a half months, the owner tried *Idealizing* the Process.

First, he *Idealized* the land in all its details. And at once a new thought came: If this land is not now valuable as a residence site, certainly there are other uses for it; and since Divine Spiritual Source, knows all uses, the idea of another use will come to me.

Second, he *Idealized* the changes in its condition at different seasons of the year and, hurrah, another new thought he had not thought before: Since the land was in a hollow and the moisture of the surrounding land drains into it, it is green many more months a year than surrounding land, an important condition in dry California, and hence it is *Ideal* for truck-gardening.

Third, he *Idealized* his activities in relation to it and to the bankers. Since Divine Spiritual Source, is all Process, He must know many ways of convincing a banker's mind. Hence a third new thought: Many people talk to bankers about the value of their lands; I'll do something besides talk to make my banker realize the value of this land as a truck garden plot. So, in one day, he called upon three different owners of truck-gardens, and got three separate offers to buy his land, although the best price offered was less than the owner wished to accept. But as the sum offered was much more than the mortgage, it made the banker Itself take new notice and even he had a new thought, a very difficult operation for a banker. His new thought was: Even if this land is not valuable for a residence site at present, it must be valuable for a truck-garden plot, if three prominent truck-gardeners want to buy it; and if they are willing to pay what they've offered, a $10,000 mortgage is certainly safe.

So the deal was closed. Two and a half months had been spent in *Idealizing* the Thing Desired, and at the end of the time it was still "desired"; three days were spent in *Idealizing* the Process, and at the end of the seventy-two hours the thing was done. *Idealizing the Thing Desired* leads you to repeat old thoughts;

Idealizing **the Process** leads you from one new thought to another new thought.

"*I shut my eyes in order to see.*"

~ *Paul Gauguin*" ~

TESTIMONIAL:
MY BEST SALE EVER

"I have been in sales my entire career. I sell products that are usable and require reorders. I have been with my company for 8 years, and I have never placed higher than 18th out of 68 in the group of salespeople in my division.

I read Ideals into Reality and worked with a Simple Keys Coach. This year I am #7 in my division.

Here is what I used to do:

(1) I would receive my quota for the year from my boss.

(2) I would write my quota on my calendar to look at when I was at my desk.

(3) I made appointments and sold whenever I could. I fought traffic to each appointment and missed some of them because I would be so late.

(4) I complained to the other salesreps how hard this job was.

(5) I took reorders and established a few new accounts during the year.

(6) I met with my boss quarterly to discuss how far off my quota my sales were at the time.

(7) I would scramble at the end of each quarter and at the end of the year to get as close to my quota as possible. I seldom exceeded my quota.

Here is what I did this year that made the difference:

(1) I took the Simple Keys class.

(2) I read the books suggested – Ideals into Reality being one of them.

(3) I consulted with a Simple Keys coach to talk about

the changes I wanted to make in my sales and income.

(4) I received my quota for the year from my boss. I discussed with my boss the quota he gave me and discussed how meeting this quota was possible. I made an agreement to meet with him weekly to Idealize my accomplishments.

(5) I sat at my desk and Idealized myself reaching my quota. I Idealized the acknowledgements from my boss. I immediately heard all the reasons in my head why this would not happen. I used the Observe & Overwrite Keys to work through these old messages.

(6) I used the free-flow Key to write all the names of my prospects and customers. I Idealized each one of them gladly buying more from me this year, and getting more benefit for themselves because of it.

(7) I wrote out my Ideal sales accomplishment in full detail and recorded it to a MP3, so I could hear myself talk about it in my car when I was in traffic, or when at

home relaxing. It was the first thing I played in the morning so I could hear myself describe my Ideal and I Idealized it in my mind and body at the same time.

(8) I followed the chapter on 5 minutes a day and read my Ideal 3 times every day. I Idealized it every time.

(9) Before I made a sales call, I Idealized the meeting, my presentation, the answers to the questions and Idealized the sale with a happy customer.

(10) Before I left for an appointment, I Idealized the meeting, my presentation, the answers to the questions and Idealized Ideal the sale with a happy customer.

(11) On the drive to the appointment, I Idealized the meeting, my presentation, the answers to the questions and Idealized the sale with a happy customer.

(12) I was more relaxed during my sales calls and more times than not, I made the sale exactly as I had Idealized it.

(13) Every time I made a new sale, I called my boss and told him my progress and my next plan of action.

(14) I only talked to my boss and my Keys coach about my Ideals.

(15) I paid attention to my gut thinking, surprise messages, unexpected new prospects. I followed my gut feelings, and found new ways to present myself and my products.

(16) I called my Keys coach anytime I felt stuck or frustrated.

(17) My first quarter, I met my bosses quota. A first! The first quarter used to be my hardest, just to get started. I reset my Ideal for the next quarter to exceed my boss's quota.

(18) My second quarter, I sold 15% more than my bosses quota. I reset my Ideal for the next quarter to be bigger than the second quarter. I was on a roll.

(19) I got overconfident and started to only Idealize sporadically.

I started having doubts if I could do it, maybe the first two quarters were just luck. I didn't work with my coach, and missed a few weekly meetings with my box. I told him I was to busy.

(20) My third quota I missed my bosses quota by 8%. Even though I was still ahead for the year, I was disappointed in myself. I got angry with myself, the message in the Ideals into Reality book, my Keys coach, and even my boss for giving me such a high quota. I felt frustrated and like a failure.

(21) That same day I "accidently" ran into a friend who took the Simple Keys class with me and had also read Ideals into Reality book. I complained about how it wasn't working and how frustrated and mad I was. He listened and then asked if I had called my coach. I was mad at my coach too so I hadn't. He told me how he had hit a very frustrating time increasing his income and

paying off old bills, so he called his Coach and let her have and earful. She listened to him and then suggested he just give the effort for one day and then call her back. That day she told him to go one more day and call her if he needed her help. One day at a time. He said he got back on track, and told me it might work for me.

(22) I called my coach and told her all the things going wrong. After listening, she asked me what my Ideal was. I had trouble answering that question. She suggested I look in my daily log for what I had done during the first two quarters that I was not doing now. And if I saw any difference, perhaps I might do some of those previous efforts just for one day, and see what happens. I looked in my log and saw I had stopped Idealizing and embodying my Ideal goal. Instead I had been daydreaming and procrastinating. I had stopped meeting with my boss and Idealizing my goal together. I had stopped getting support from my coach. I had slipped back into my old habits.

(23) I reread Ideals into Reality. I reread my Simple Keys journal.

(24) I sat down with my boss, took responsibility for not keeping my weekly appointment agreement with him. We discussed the possibilities of how to make this my best year ever. I recommitted to meeting him every week to discuss my progress.

(25) I called my Coach and she helped me to clarify my Ideal so I could write it out. I signed up for the Keys email support program.

(26) I sat at my desk and Idealized myself exceeding my boss's quota and having my best year ever. I Idealized the acknowledgements I would receive from my boss and the surprise from the other salespeople.

(27) I used the Observe & Overwrite Keys to work through the old messages that showed up again. This time there were new self-defeating messages that I got during this last quarter.

(28) I used the free-flow Key to write all the names of my prospects and customers. Some I had sold already this year and some had already told me they had no more budget. I Idealized each one of them gladly buying more and getting more benefit it for themselves because of it. When I did this, I had amazing thoughts about what products to show them and what benefits there were for them, that I had not explained before.

(29) I wrote out my new Ideal sales goal in full detail and recorded it to a newMP3. I played it in my car when I was in traffic, and when at home relaxing. It was the first thing I played in the morning. When I listened to myself describe my Ideal, I also Idealized it Ideal it at the same time.

(30) I read my Ideal 3 times every day.

(31) Before I made a sales call, I Idealized the meeting complete with a happy customer.

(32) Before I left for an appointment, I Idealized the meeting complete with a happy customer.

(33) On the drive to the appointment, I Idealized the meeting complete with a happy customer.

(34) I made more sales and new customers exactly as I Idealized it.

(35) Every time I made a new sale, I called my boss and told him my progress and my next plan of action.

(36) I only talked to my boss and my Simple Keys coach about my Ideals.

(37) I paid attention and followed my gut feelings. I took action on new ideas. I re-read some of my own sales literature and found new ways to present myself and my products.

(38) I called my Coach anytime I felt stuck or frustrated.

(39) I exceeded the yearly quota my boss gave me by 139%, and I finished my sales year at #7.

(40) At our sales and awards meeting I was given a trophy for the first time. I was seated at the table with the other top sales reps. I was asked to talk for 15 minutes to the sales group about how I had accomplished such an increase in sales this year. When I sat down, some of the other reps at my table told me that what I did with my Idealizing was similar to what they do all the time. They either learned it from another class, from a mentor, from a book or from their parents. For them it is like a second nature, they do it naturally. So what seems like an effort to me right now will become easier and a real part of me if I will keep doing it. They told me about some of the books they read. Some of them were on my recommended reading list. I got invited to join a master mind group.

Other areas of my life changed for the better this year too. It has been a great year for me.

The best sale I made this year was to myself. *To sell myself into take a chance on making a change; to commit to what I had learned and take responsibility for my thoughts, words and actions.*

This next year I am aiming at the top 5. I will be re-reading my log and doing the same things I did this year that proved to work for me." ~ *Arthur Mansfield, Palo Alto, CA* ~

IDEALIZING PROPERTY VALUES, POSITIONS AND ADVANCEMENT

CHAPTER 20

LAND VALUES INCREASE 400% IN FOUR DAYS

One of our writers has emphasized the policy of using what you have to get what you want. It is a policy of failure if you do not *Idealize* that which you have. If, however, you *Idealize* the thing you have to use and the process of using it, it becomes a sure road to success and great success. Values are increased only by *Idealizing*.

But how can the mind of itself and within itself, by a mere process of thinking, increase the value of anything?

Especially, let us say, the value of such a thing as a piece of land, of real estate? Certainly, it seems that its value depends not at all on what we think about it. You know what land is; but, do you know what value is? Certainly, value is nothing material. If mind did not distinguish between a diamond and a piece of coal and give special value to the former because of our desire for beauty, the material of the diamond would be no more valuable than the material of a piece of coal of the same size. If there were no mental conception regarding the purity of the diamond and no desire to possess it and use it as decoration, diamonds would possess no more value than pebbles.

Now let us consider the *Idealizing* of the value of a piece of land so that the process increased its value in four days from less than $200 an acre to $1,000 an acre. The land, of which I write, is situated in eastern Pennsylvania near a very beautiful lake some distance from railroads. It was purchased twenty-four years ago as farmland at less than $15 an acre. It was left as part of an estate to two nephews. The younger one became of age in 1919 and the land was offered for sale. They desired to obtain $200 an acre for it and felt that, if they could sell it at that price, they would be very lucky. Many things have happened in the last twenty-four years. The land is still far from the railroad but every foot of land around the little lake has been purchased by millionaires from Philadelphia and New York. In fact, since 1919 they have spent $3,000,000 in general improvement of this millionaires' colony in addition to the money spent on individual estates.

The land of the two nephews, however, was not of great value. The acreage was not large enough for a great estate and the land was not good as farmland. In no sense did it lead surrounding land in value. Those who knew the land thought it ought to be worth $200 an acre, but, as the months went by, it was not sold. The nephews were anxious to realize on their land; they wished to go into business, and knowing me, they called one day to ask for help. I *Idealized* it as farmland and saw its uselessness. In fact, it had been neglected so long that it would take two or three years to bring it back to normal condition. Then I *Idealized* it as a site for a country estate of a wealthy man. But I saw it would not do for that. It was not large enough. Next, I *Idealized* the entire colony of millionaires about it; I *Idealized* its nearness to New York and Philadelphia; I *Idealized* the people in the city who desired homes; I *Idealized* human nature, realizing that there were many cultured people of limited means who desired to live near very wealthy people who would enjoy life in a community of such people.

Consequently out of the cosmos there came to my mind the *Ideal* of making this land a little park divided into forty little home plots of one acre each. The nephews and I drew up this plan. We had given added value to the actual land by creating an *Idealized* use of it, a vision of a little park among the millionaires, for forty families each with its own little country home. The first result was accomplished within forty-eight hours. The plan was presented to a real estate man in New York City. At once he wished to buy the entire plot at $300 an acre. But the nephews had seen a vision. The

Idealization had given value to their land and they refused. The real estate man offered $400, and then $500 an acre for it.

The second result was that within four days the nephews were offered $1,000 an acre for the first plot that was to be sold. And why? The land was exactly the same land it had been a week before, but value had been added by *Idealizing* a little community of forty cultured families living near a colony of millionaires, and value had also been given to it by creating a desire for such homes. These two factors, the mental plan and the desire created, gave a greatly increased value (from $200 to $1,000 an acre) in four days. Because of the plan and the desire created in the minds of those to whom the plan was given, this run-down, neglected farmland led in value all the other farmland, even though the other farmlands were improved and cultivated. This was possible because this land was hilly and rolling and partly wooded Therefore other farmland could not compete with this as plots for homes.

Moreover, in value this land within four days after the plan was made and presented was worth just five hundred percent more than the lands of the great estates surrounding them. It was worth more because it could be purchased in small plots, while the owners of the estates would not consider selling an acre or even ten acres of the land they owned. Hence this land, which, four days before the plan was conceived by *Idealization* as at the tail of land values, became the leader of land values in comparison with farm land value and that of the great estates.

Whenever you wish to increase the value of anything you have to sell, add mental effort by sane *Idealization* that fits the best use that can be made of the thing. Whenever you wish to give a predominant value to anything, *Idealize* a plan and create a desire for it in such a way that the thing you have to sell leads all other things near it or approximately like it.

Thus, by actual practice, you prove that all value is of mind and thus that all value is of Divine Spiritual

Source. The value of that, which you possess, depends upon the sanely *Idealized* concept with which you endow it and the desire you create in other minds for the honest value you have given it.

CHAPTER 21

VALUELESS WET LANDS MADE PROFITABLE BY IDEALIZATION

Strange as it seems, yet it is true, **greatly** increased value can be given to land, even to useless land possessing no market value at all, by such *Ideals* as love and service, the values of which are apparently so distinct and separate from the values of land. But values of love and service cannot be connected with the values of land unless the process of relating the two factors is *Idealized*.

Frankly, I do not know whether the father and mother, concerned with the story I am writing, recognize *Idealization* or not. But one thing is certain, whether they recognize it or not, the great success they made in using a little plot of useless low wet land to provide college education for their three children is the result of *Idealization*.

The story begins twenty-two years ago. Soon after they were married, the father of the young wife gave her a little plot of wetland, seemingly quite useless except for water bugs and sand flies. It was on the Rhode Island coast, off the main road, in an out-of-the-way place. Even today it is twelve miles from a railway station. On the plot, the father built for his daughter a little cottage, to which the young married couple could go for the summertime.

During the next few years three children were born to them. The mother and father were poor. It was possible to carry the children through grammar school and high school, but how to pay their way through college was a problem! The hearts of the mother and father were filled with a consuming desire, a desire to give each of their children a college education. Their

173

minds were practical minds. Hence, they looked about to see what they had that could be used to help provide a means of sending their children to college.

I presume when they first thought of the wetland at the seashore and the little cottage there, in the out-of-the-way place, it seemed only an object of expense to them, certainly not the means of an income sufficient to provide three college educations. But they did something with this real thing they had. They *Idealized* it. They may have done this consciously; they may have done it unconsciously. But, they did it.

Instead of thinking of the land as an out-of-the-way wet place to which few people wished to go, they *Idealized* it as a place of peaceful seclusion to which a certain class of people would wish to go for a rest. Such *Idealization* recognizes Divine Spiritual Source, as Wisdom. It was adapted to the place and the conditions, to themselves and to their pocketbooks. I was there one July. There were no glass-screened porches, no casinos, no ornamented boardwalks, and no vain show

174

of life. But there was life itself! The people visiting there were real people. There was freedom of action. There was fellowship and the spirit of love and service. Also there was rest.

The father and mother had made it pay. They had made it pay from year to year, which means they had rendered such good service, such *Idealized* service for the prices charged, that visitors returned year after year. They have succeeded. The three children have been given college educations and this in itself is sufficient proof of their success. And yet there is something greater than this. The father and mother each summer are giving a spiritual education to a hundred or more different guests who see Divine Spiritual Source's *Idealization* of service in action.

CHAPTER 22

OBTAINING IN REALITY THE IDEAL POSITION YOU DESIRE

Be very sure of that. He is everything that exists, not only in the mental and spiritual world, but everything that really exists in the material world.

If you think and plan in ideas and act in accord with them, be certain that you will leave out some essential factor of your effort and probably fail to attain that which you desire. In thinking and planning to secure the position you desire, or to create a position for yourself, your plans may not become realities if you fail to *Idealize* and use any one of the factors.

Here is a little incident: that of a young man who changed in a few weeks from making thirty-five dollars a week and working eight hours a day to making five hundred dollars a month working but four hours a day. I met him by accident; no, not by accident, but by Divine Spiritual Source's designing.

It happened thus: One Sunday afternoon I went up into that section of the wild north end of Central Park where one can imagine oneself in the deep woods. I stretched myself on the ground and, reclining against a big rock, started to read. A young couple had come up from the other side and had stopped for a moment and begun to talk. I thought they would move on in a moment, so I kept still. But instead, they sat down on the very rock against which I was reclining. "You see, dear, "the young man said," you've accepted a mere trailer. I'm just pulled along by business, that's all. I advance as it advances, but I am not the racer you think me; I am not even a flivver. I can't even see a chance of spurting ahead of the others." "But you're so wonderful and such a good stenographer," she protested. "Someone will find out your real worth."

"I am only one in 40,000," he answered.

Startled, astounded, they jumped up and looked around, for from the other side of the rock had come these words: "Well, you blubbering young Romeo, why don't you stop thinking of things as they are and work them out as they ought to be?" It was my own voice and it astonished me almost as much as it astounded them. I realized I had "thought out loud" and determined to make the best of it.

Getting up, I said, "I am sorry; I was here reading. You came up and I could not help but hear."

"Well, I'll be damned," said the young man. "A good greeting, that," I replied, "and an introduction also; I offer my services as business counselor, no fees, it is Sunday you know," and I held out my hand. The girl smiled and I smiled; and then, he smiled and grasped my hand. We sat down and I talked about *Idealizing* things as they ought to be, of the necessity of avoiding dreamy visions, of pinning one's *Idealization* down to fit the possibilities.

"But, what do you mean by this *Idealization*?" he said. "Just this," I replied. "*Idealization* is the process of establishing a perfect standard in the mind. That means considering every part; the individual, the means at hand, the place, the work itself, the other people concerned, the conditions and the time: making a composite whole out of all the ideas.

"Apply these to your case. You are a good stenographer. I accept you at your own valuation, but you are no better than a thousand others, perhaps, five thousand others in New York City. If you can make yourself stand out from all the rest as rendering a service they cannot render, would you be able to command almost any income you pleased? " "Well, I should say I could."

"Can you, by merely bettering your work, make yourself stand out as a stenographer above all other stenographers?" "Perhaps I could, if I worked ten years at it; but then, a thousand others could do the same." "That, then, is one part of the idea considered, and discarded.

"Next, take up the idea of place. You live in New York City. How long have you lived here?" "All my life." "Have you ever *Idealized* it?" "I don't know what you mean." "Well have you ever attempted to think of New York City in a big way, to vision all the possibilities within itself and its relationship to the rest of the country? Close your eyes. Picture New York City with its millions of people, its hundreds of thousands of offices, its tens of thousands of big business men and bankers and shippers doing business with all parts of the world. Vision businessmen coming to New York City from all over the country, from all the rest of the world. Do you see New York City as a great opportunity for a business stenographer? Do you see the place as offering the great opportunity?" "Yes," he answered," I do."

"Now, *Idealize* your own work. I heard you say you were a mere stenographer. Think of your work as it actually is by picturing its *Ideal* side. Picture it as a perfect whole. Vision its importance. Visualize what would happen if, in one moment, all stenographers should forget everything they knew about stenography, and all knowledge of stenography should be lost. Imagine the conditions that would exist if all businessmen and all their clerks were compelled to make all records and handle all correspondence by handwriting. Has your *Idealization* given you a realization of the importance of stenographic work?" "Yes," he replied, monosyllabically.

"There are still to be considered the other people concerned, those needing services the existing conditions, and the time. What class of people is most in need of stenography?" "Why, business men, of course." "Are the needs of these business men met every day by the work of the stenographers in their offices?" "Yes" "Are there any business men in New York City who do not have offices?" "Why, none of importance." "When

181

you *Idealized* New York City as a business center, did you not vision big business men coming here from all over the country?" "Certainly." "Do you know there are about 200,000 of these men in New York City every single day of the year?" "Is that so!" "Have these men need of stenographic services?" "Yes, but they go to public stenographers or hotel stenographers. I don't see any special chance there." "Neither do I. Frankly, I don't know what the solution is going to be; but I do know that if we continue *Idealizing* every single factor and keep them all in mind, we will see a new relationship and a new need. It always works out something."

"Let us take the next point: conditions of service." "Are you ever asked to work overtime?" "Not often; but sometimes I work till ten or eleven o'clock when the boss wants to get out special letters or telegrams for the midnight mail." "Then the conditions of stenographic service are such that business men do now and then, even those living in New York City, wish service which, under ordinary conditions, is not rendered.

"This brings us to the subject of time. It is clear that stenographic service is rendered in the daytime; it is also clear that it is not rendered at night. Even hotel stenographers do not work later than nine or ten o'clock. Does that give you any idea? "Yes, but nothing I can get hold of; nothing I can actually use!" "Well, let's drop it, now. Think of all these yourself, the means, the work, the other people, the conditions, the time, over and over again tonight. *Idealize* every one of the factors. Don't omit a single one. Come to see me tomorrow night. Here's my address."

The next night he came. He was a different man. He was no longer a stenographer; he was a creator. More than that, he was an inspired creator. A new idea, a new thought, an inspiration, had come to him. This is what he did: he organized a stenographic night service between nine in the evening and one in the morning for businessmen coming to the city for a day or two. For this service, at such a time, he was able to charge twice the price of a public day stenographer. The service rendered to a big business man who, having settled business affairs in the early evening, wished to get off contracts or letters or telegraphic instructions after the hotel stenographic offices bad closed, was worth the price. By *Idealizing* the time of rendering service, he made his stenographic work surpass and lead all other stenographic services in the city.

A little home was bought and furnished; they're married now!

CHAPTER 23

ADVANCEMENT DEPENDS UPON IDEALIZING ITS PROCESS

Your work in the world is performed in one or more of three fields:

(1) work with things,

(2) work with words,

(3) work with people.

In each of these fields of work, there are thousands and thousands, who serve earnestly and loyally, work efficiently year after year, and yet, the advancement they

185

desire is not attained. Are you one of these? If so, why do you not win the advancement for which you strive so earnestly? Because you fail (1) to make yourself a leader in the work you are doing; or fail (2) to prepare yourself for the field of service you desire to enter. If you make things better than others make, or if you make things more rapidly or more efficiently or more beautifully than others do, you lead them in the work you and they are doing and your leadership brings advancement. But advancement does not come merely because of good work, it must be better work than others do, better than all others about you do. If you make yourself a leader in any field of work, work with things, words or people, you are given advancement.

Now, the next factor: your preparation for work in another field of service. It is in this that most earnest workers fail. To attain this kind of advancement, advancement from one field of work to another, earnest and efficient work, loyalty, skill and years of experience are of little value unless you *Idealize* the process of advancing from the field in which you are working to the field in which you wish to work. Even years of preparation are almost useless unless the process of preparation has been *Idealized.*

Take, for instance, the case of John, Old John, they now call him. Forty-four years ago he was a young machinist learning his trade. He was energetic, ambitious and hopeful. He worked well. At night he studied mechanics at home. Later he went to a night school and studied mechanical drawing. Yet he did not neglect his work: his machine was always in good condition; he worked faithfully and well; he turned out a greater amount of work per day and did better work than any other man in the shop. But he was not promoted. Today he is still an expert machinist and they call him Old John, expert old John! He certainly had an *Ideal,* a worthy, ambitious, definite *Ideal.* The hope of his boyhood was to become boss of the shop and then foreman in some larger shop and ultimately the head of a department. Yet with all his skillful work and all his earnest effort and study and application, he has failed.

But Divine Spiritual Source is Good; the world is good; and old John was given just reward for everything he did! He worked well and got the reward for this, good pay. He trained himself to be skilled and rapid in his work and got his reward for this. When piece-work pay was adopted, he received a larger sum per day than any other machinist in the shop; in fact, more than any other machinist in the city. He studied mechanics and took excellent care of his machine and got his reward for this. The highest bonus paid for the least wear and tear of a machine. He served long and loyally and got his reward for this: the highest extra Christmas bonus based proportionately on the number of years service.

But he was never advanced to the position of boss.

No person should be advanced to directing other people, human souls, merely because he or she is expert in operating a machine; no person should be made a teacher of children merely because he or she is an expert in shelling peas. Old John did not *Idealize* the process of advancing from his field or work, handling things, to the field he wished to enter, handling other workers. All his study of mechanics and mechanical drawing brought him a reward; it made him a better machinist; but it did not fit him to direct other workers.

Three years ago, a young man who then knew nothing whatever about any machine, started at the same shop and now he is boss. He had the same *Ideal* Old John had; the same ambition; the same zeal; the same energy. He also studied mechanics and mechanical drawing and trained himself to run a machine expertly; but he wished to get into the field of directing other workers so he *Idealized* the process and adapted his preparation to it. Hence, he studied other workers: during the noon hour, he watched them; he got clues of the impulses and desires that impelled each to do things or to refuse to do things; he watched the bosses also to learn how they handled the other workers; he observed their successes and their failures; he *Idealized* Itself in the process of handling the other workers; he learned how to get them to do things without antagonizing them; and soon, well, he is now foreman of the shop.

Advancement comes to those who advance themselves. If you feel a little hurt and a little sullen and a little resentful because you have not been advanced, made a leader in other lines of work, look to yourself. First, *Idealize* just exactly the type of work you are doing now; second, *Idealize* the type of work you want to do; third, *Idealize* the process of preparation necessary to fit yourself to do the type of work you want to do. Be truthful to yourself: have you prepared yourself in the right way or have you merely done your work well and asked for advancement? If you foolishly think you can fit yourself to direct people by making yourself an expert dressmaker, don't blame anyone but yourself. Divine Spiritual Source, gave you mind; use it! Not only effort, but mind effort, intelligent mind effort, *Idealized* intelligent mind effort, makes you worthy of advancement.

TESTIMONIAL:
MY IDEAL HOME

"After reading How To Turn Your Desires And Ideals Into Reality, I realized that I have been using this process in my life for small and insignificant things with clear results. Such as planning my daughters birthday party; planning our vacation; "seeing" my drive safely in traffic; finding parking spaces, and so many other small ways.

After this eye-opener, I committed to using this same aware process in finding, buying and moving into my new home.

I had a budget to spend, and had several professional real estate salespersons tell me that what I was seeking would cost several thousand more than my budget. With each rejection I re-focused on my Ideal home, and also included the Ideal real estate person to work with.

With each Ideal of my home, I also Idealized the ease of packing, the ease of moving and the ease of unpacking. While my realtor did her job to find my Ideal home for me, I started packing. I Idealized each room in my new home. As I packed, I placed every item in the box, clearly marked for its new destination. In the past I usually just packed items according to what room they were currently in, not the rooms they were going into at my new location. I used a computer designer program to sketch room layouts with my furniture and accessories.

5 weeks and 2 days after I wrote down and clearly Idealized my new home, I received a call from my realtor. She thought she had found my Ideal home. The home she showed me was not my Ideal home. It had some very nice features, but not what I had Idealized. But, when we were getting ready to leave the home after viewing, the owner of the house next door stopped us and asked to talk to my realtor. He wanted to list his home for sale. I asked for permission to come on the tour of his home, and the minute I stepped through the front door, I new I was in my Ideal home.

I contained my enthusiasm as much as possible, and gave my realtor a look to tell her that this was the home for me. She negotiated a price with the owner, and when I signed the contract it was for the exact priced I had Idealized. I negotiated and got a savings because my realtor was both the listing and the selling agent. The seller was motivated to sell and I was pre-qualified by my bank, so the negotiation on the final price was simple, and it was exactly as I had Idealized. I got the short escrow I wanted, and I was completely packed when the movers arrived.

The movers put the furniture, boxes and artwork in the rooms appropriate to my packing. So when they left, I was already more moved in than I had ever been. The movers had placed my rugs and my furniture exactly where I had sketched. I tipped them to help me hang the artwork. All I had to do was unpack the boxes and since I had packed everything according to my Ideal, I knew which boxes to unpack first and where to place everything. I was completely unpacked within a week after the movers left. This was undoubtedly the easiest real estate purchase and move I had every done.

The process I had been using for little things in my life proved to work on big and significant things too."
~ Karen Moore, Woodland Hills, CA ~

HEALING
OF
SO-CALLED
INCURABLE
CASES

CHAPTER 24

MAKING A SOLID ANKLE JOINT FLEXIBLE AND USABLE

In the matter of spiritual healing let me make myself clear to you at the beginning of this section. Spiritual healing recognizes Divine Spiritual Source as All and Everything and puts the truth into practice, using everything, but everything only when *Idealized*. Spiritual healing does include material means, but material means only as spiritual manifestation. I am well aware that spiritual theorists differ with me in this: they say that depending upon material means limits my thought of Divine Spiritual Source. There are two mistakes in this statement. First, spiritual healing does not depend upon material means but it does use them and use them only when *Idealized*. Second, I answer that those who criticize, limit their thought for they first insist that the patient accept the truth that Divine Spiritual Source is All and Good and secondly, insist that he or she must not use the truth that Divine Spiritual Source is All because some of Divine Spiritual Source's manifestations are not good.

Having read the three Chapters of the section entitled The Spirit of Matter, you now know that denying that so-called matter is a manifestation of Divine Spiritual Source is the same as denying that infinity of space, infinite attractive energy and infinite activity are of Divine Spiritual Source. In those three Chapters you learned that density of matter is but Divine Spiritual Source's infinite space, that solidity of matter is but Divine Spiritual Source's infinite attractive energy, and that matter is but etheric aliveness, infinite energy ever present.

I, then, in Spiritual Healing, adhere in practice to the truth that Divine Spiritual Source is All and use not only Divine Spiritual Source's spiritual *Ideal* but Divine

Spiritual Source's spiritual manifestation as well. That is, Divine Spiritual Source as All and Everything!

Take first a case of healing that has to do with that which is most difficult to handle: the changing of bone structure. When I was three years old my left foot and ankle were crushed between the rollers of a one-horse sugar mill. The foot and the leg, half way to the knee, were so badly injured that, when the rollers were reversed, it was necessary to lay me sidewise on a board to prevent the crushed foot from dropping off. The doctors molded it back into form as best they could and put it into a cast. But the irregular bones of the ankle were so crushed and mashed that they grew together as one single solid bone. When the cast was taken off, I could not move the ankle at all; I could not flex it any more than you can bend the bone of your arm half way between elbow and shoulder.

As the leg from knee to toes was as stiff as a carved piece of wood, it was necessary to use a cane or a crutch and to hunch my whole body upward in order to swing the other leg forward. Today, I can move the left foot up and down at the ankle as easily as I can move my right foot. I do not even limp! My step is springy and certain. Friends say that my walk is more like that of a man of thirty than that of a man of sixty-five. Certainly, with the small bones of my ankle grown together as one solid bone, I was compelled to do something with my consciousness of the "solidity" of matter.

To get rid of the idea that matter is COMPACT, DENSE and SOLID is the first step in all healing. So long as you think of a cancer, or a tumor, or an abnormal bone growth, as compact solid matter, so long will you doubt the power of mind and spirit to change it. Throughout all the ages, individuals have been healed by prayer, faith, mind, love and spirit. Each such case proves it can be done. Yet today, not one person of each twenty million of the world's population is healed directly by such methods. We cannot account for this, by asserting that the world does not know that Divine Spiritual Source has healed. We cannot account for it by asserting that millions do not wish to be made well by spiritual healing. If, at any time during the ages, we had held to the truth that Divine Spiritual Source is All and known that matter is spiritual manifestation, the knowledge of the results of our spiritual healing would have swept the world and everyone would now accept and use them.

We have *Ideals* of Divine Spiritual Source, spirit, and spiritual healing. We have no *Ideal* of matter, the thing to be healed. Our failures have been due to our partial and very mistaken ideas of matter. Some have tried to get around matter by calling it an illusion. Think of matter as an illusion as much as you please but, if you have a cancer on the end of your nose, deep in your heart you know that you cannot deny that your mind recognizes that that cancer is there!

So long as you call matter an illusion, you admit there is something to be called an illusion; and that something makes you doubt to one degree or another the possibility of the healing. Others try to get around matter, by denying its existence. So long as you find it necessary to deny matter, your very denial is your admission that there is something to deny. Is it consistent to deny the existence of the matter we call a cancer and then to turn our minds topsy-turvy in a second and demand that supply be manifested as matter in the form of money and means of material existence, food, clothing, houses, etc.

Demanding the presence of one kind of matter and denying the existence of another indicates a partial but not a complete conception of spiritual manifestation. And so long as our conception of truth is incomplete, we heal now and then, but not always. Christ never denied matter. He changed its manifestation by spiritual power: water to wine, for instance. But He never denied the water or the wine. He increased the number of loaves and fishes and, in teaching His disciples the lesson to be drawn from the miracle, He called specific attention to matter for He emphasized the fact that there were but a few loaves and fishes before the change and many thousands afterwards.

Divine Spiritual Source is All: Everything that is true in spiritual existence is true in material existence and vice versa. If Divine Spiritual Source is holy, then all of His manifestations are holy. "If the root be holy," writes Paul, "so are the branches." Your body is composed of cells. Cells are composed of atoms and atoms of electrons. Christ did not deny the existence of the body; He called it a temple-a place of holiness. Cells, atoms and electrons are Divine Spiritual Source, in manifestation, just as much as thought is! Divine Spiritual Source is ALL.

How did I change a solid anklebone to a flexible and usable joint? First, I *Idealized* matter exactly as I have done for you in the three Chapters of the section entitled "The Spirit of Matter." Read them again, read them a thousand times if necessary, for the idea that matter is dense, solid and motionless has been accepted millions of times by your mind. What, then, if it does take a thousand readings to dispel the mistaken ideas?

Second, after *Idealizing* matter in general, I *Idealized* the particular matter of the ankle joint. I knew it was composed of cells, each composed of molecules, millions of them. I *Idealized* a molecule as it truly exists, a mere etheric spherical space in which atoms whirl at a tremendous rate. I *Idealized* the atoms of every molecule of that bone structure, knowing each to be but a smaller etheric spherical space composed of electrons. Then I *Idealized* the bone structure as composed of electrons. I *Idealized* these elections as being far, far apart; I *Idealized* them as moving at stupendous speeds; I *Idealized* the electron itself as only an infinitely small whirling hole in space. Then my anklebone became infinite space energy, formed and held together by infinite attractive energy, no more dense nor solid than infinitely active holes in space.

Was this all I did? No, this was but my *Ideal* of the substance of which the ankle joint is composed and of the process of infinite energy in operation. Hence, third, I *Idealized* every process and means of developing muscles to move the ankle and of developing nerves to move the muscles; I rubbed the ankle; pulled it; pressed it; tried to turn it this way and that; used every means of which I could conceive, anything that might induce motion. Never, however, did I for a moment think of it as dense, solid and motionless. I knew that bone to be infinite energy. I knew that my soul could control and direct that energy; that it could form, re-form, and create anew the bone structure itself. I knew the structure, as all great scientists were then beginning to realize, to be only infinite energy under my control.

No matter what it is to be healed, your first step is to *Idealize* matter; *Idealize* it as it truly is, made up of infinitely small, whirling holes of energy held together by the infinite attractive energy of Divine Spiritual Source. Being only infinite energy, matter can be changed by the Infinite Will and Spirit residing in each of us.

CHAPTER 25

HEALING A DYING MAN OF CANCER OF THE STOMACH

This is a case of healing illustrating the *Idealized* Process of using Divine Spiritual Source's Intelligence discriminatively. Many mental theorists also object to this. They refuse to think particular *Ideals* of details, asserting that Divine Spiritual Source's general concept of truth and perfect health are sufficient. Failures in healing would be lessened if we were wise enough to realize that Divine Spiritual Source, Itself was unable to create anything of value in manifestation except by the use of discriminative intelligence.

Divine Spiritual Source, first created our world by general concept; but what was the result? It was "without form and void." Then, Divine Spiritual Source used the discriminative intelligence and separated the light from the darkness, the firmament from the earth, the waters from the land, etc. Let us not be so unwise as to depend upon mere general concepts of truth. Hold them, if you will, till you are blind and gray, and your manifestations will still be "formless, and void."

During the last seventy years spiritual healing has been characterized by three distinct stages: The first stage did not truly represent even the thought taught at that time, for many persons, with but a vague idea of what it was all about and a wish to do good, set themselves up as healers. It was the stage of denial and in some cases absurd denial.

I remember well the time when, if one went to such an uninformed or misinformed healer for treatment for headache, the healer would say, "But how can you have a headache, you have no head?" Then came the second stage of spiritual healing. In this the denial became the less important and the recognition of great spiritual truths the more important. When specific application was then tried, it tended toward materialism. Now, we are *Idealizing* every step in the process and making it spiritual. Hence it adds to, rather than detracts from, the great spiritual truths.

We now come to the third stage of spiritual healing, the recognition of particular truths and the specific application of them. We are advancing. We know that All is Divine Spiritual Source in action and practice as well as in general statement.

Let me give you a case that demonstrates the effectiveness of specific application after the failure of general affirmation. It is the case of a man who was thirty-five years old when the healing took place, afflicted with cancer of the stomach and said to be dying at the time. Four specialists had treated him and at the time the case was brought to my attention he was to be operated upon in two days. It was his wife who came to me. The man himself was thirty-two miles away in a hospital; too weak even to feed himself. He had been ill for some years. First there had been medical treatment, X-rays, diet, serum and, when these had failed, he had tried suggestion, mental healing, divine healing, Christian Science.

At first it seemed impossible for me to take the case. Affairs prevented my going to the man. I realized, although his wife was trying to give the correct *Ideal* of his mental condition, she might not know it well enough to give me the information necessary to make specific application successful. I did know, however, of two of the healers; who had been trying to help him. I called them on the telephone and found they had been treating for health, life and wholeness. Now these conditions were exactly what was desired as an end to be attained. The man wanted to be healthy; he wanted to be whole; he wanted to live. These conditions were exactly what the healers desired. He had faith and the healers had faith, and yet he had not been healed.

Hanging up the telephone, I turned to the wife and questioned her. She did not know exactly what I was driving at, and neither did I; but I found out that the phrases most frequently used by her husband were: "Oh, I'm so tired"; or, "I am too tired to do that," or, "I am so tired, I cannot try." This, then, was the stumbling block. It was fatigue. As long as this consciousness continued, it contradicted the truths of health, life and wholeness, for one who is healthy and whole is not so burdened with fatigue. I decided to use the specific truth strength as the truth that would lead to the end desired.

This was at four o'clock in the afternoon. The wife left me and I at once spent a half hour and another half hour at midnight, *Idealizing* Divine Spiritual Source, as All Energy, All Vitality and All Life, *Idealizing* Energy and Vitality and Life and Strength as flowing through that man's body. The first result: Twenty-three hours later a tall, thin, white-faced man walked into my office. His first words were: "Mrs. W. was here yesterday to see you about a cancer case." I looked at the man, noted his white face, and thought: "Good Lord, he's evidently her brother. The husband must be dead or she would have come herself." I asked him to be seated and he said: "I am very grateful to you. My wife told me that you would center all thought upon strength, and I am astounded at the results." If he was astounded, I, myself, was dumfounded. The man had literally picked up his bed and walked, had dressed himself with little help and had come thirty-two miles by train to see me.

My treatment was not one bit more of truth than the treatment of the healers who had previously worked for him. The one difference was this, that the wife and I had made a specific application, discerned WHAT truth must first be brought to consciousness and used that truth to lead to the end desired. I am certain from this and a thousand other cases that there is never a failure when Divine Spiritual Source is recognized as wisdom, when the true mental cause is discerned and the specific application of truth is made to fit the case.

As to the second result: there is no need of elaboration; it is enough to state that within ten days the man was at work and that the healing was permanent.

CHAPTER 26

CURING THE AFTERMATH OF FORTY YEARS OF REPRESSION

What innumerable images, ideas, impulses, thoughts and feelings are pressed back and hidden in the subconsciousness of each person's mind! I remember slipping off a little rowboat pier at a Michigan summer resort about twenty years ago. To the conscious mind, it was but thirty or forty seconds from the time my head went under the water till it bobbed up again and I was helped into one of the rowboats tied to the pier. But subconsciously, I lived years: I saw the snow peaks of the Himalayas; a jungle army of African gorillas; a garden of roses in Rome; I worked out the chapters of a

213

book on a new philosophy of life; I felt passions previously unknown to me; I heard people gibbering and saw twenty or more box cars filled with dirty linen; I conceived a new play; planned to build a pyramid; and even saw the headlines of a newspaper announcing my death "in the presence of forty thousand people" when in reality there were only eight people on the pier.

Every suppression is a possible cause of an ill or failure of one kind or another, even though the conscious mind does not know that such suppression exists or that such cause is operating. To one ill of the wild animal, man has ten thousand diseases. The animal's subconsciousness is hourly expressed; but man's subconsciousness is habitually suppressed. So long as the cause is hidden in the subconsciousness, the conscious mind often fails to heal. It succeeds only when it happens to hit the nail on the head.

Let me illustrate the value of a study of hidden causes by a particular case: Twenty-one months ago a man 56 years of age came to me. His heart palpitated so badly that his physicians feared for his life week by week. He was subject also to periods of great despondency and to fits of violent temper. These had been growing worse for twenty years or more. He had been a poor boy and was now wealthy. He had faith in prayer, mental healing and Christian Science.

First, he had been treated by physicians; he had tried "change of scene," and had been hypnotized; then for years, he had relied upon mental treatment to cure him. Yet he had not been healed. As he told me the story of the sincere and earnest efforts of others to help him, I became certain that there was some cause hidden in his subconscious mind that was at the bottom of all his trouble. But his conscious mind could remember nothing that seemed to be of sufficient importance to cause so persistent a condition.

The process is this: discover the hidden cause in the subconscious mind; interpret it; and thus give the conscious mind a chance to *Idealize* and express it in normal action.

To return to our case: an analysis of the subconscious showed that the man preferred yellow, violet and old rose to other colors. He preferred opera to any other form of entertainment. In drama, he liked the villain best; but in opera, the hero. Of different voices, he liked the bass best; and of music, that of the pipe organ. In writing 900 words, anything that came into his mind beginning with the word match, he wrote smooth 27 times, harmony 42; times, heaven 37 times, flowing 11, sound 28, organ 53, father 41, hell 36, concert 42, opera 28.

Space limits me as to detail; but this is what I discovered. As a young boy, his greatest desire was to play the organ. The next strongest desire was to listen to organ music. He often went to a Catholic Church to hear the organ music. But his father was a Baptist and thrashed the boy every time he found out that the boy had been to the Catholic Church. Music aroused limitless feelings that demanded expression; but, because of his father, these were always suppressed by fear. Consequently, as means of curing him, instead of concentration on calmness and peace and control, as had been done in previous treatments, I chose Courage and Harmony in Action. This last was put in practice. The man learned to play a pipe organ. Within thirty days he was cured. In eighteen months that have since passed, he has never had an attack of blues or a fit of temper and his heart beats as normally as my own.

Divine Spiritual Source, is All Knowledge; hidden and revealed. Your subconscious mind is infinite, with the infinity of Divine Spiritual Source. Out of it all ideas, impulses and feelings you need to know will come to you. There is nothing hidden that shall not be revealed.

TESTIMONIAL:
FINALLY GETTING MY IDEAL BODY

"I watched The Secret and it motivated me to want to learn more to learn HOW to think and have it be real in my life. I read book after book and still felt I didn't have the answer I needed. Then I discovered It Works with Simple Keys and How To Turn Your Desires And Ideals Into Reality" and it's like the pieces of the puzzle started fitting together.

I have measurable results with my body, my health and my weight after applying what I learned in these two books.

For the last couple of years I would tell anyone that no matter what I did, I couldn't lose weight. I exercised when I watched TV, I worked out with a trainer 2 times week and went to the gym 3 times additional. I tried several different diets, some at the same time, and I kept putting on pounds or only losing such a minimal amount that I felt defeated.

More out of desperation of one last try than any real commitment, I decided to put what I had read to the test. So many other philosophies had told me to never look at where you are, to only look where you were going. That was hard for me to do. My realty kept hitting me in the face. I started by forcing myself to see the truth about where I was. Once I knew "my reality today", I then Idealized each step of the way and Idealized "my new reality".

The first thing I did was keep a journal of everything I ate, every exercise I did and what I was thinking about during those times. I was looking to discover if I was doing or not doing something that I could now change.

When I finally faced the truth, new thing I discovered was that when I was exercising I was complaining out loud and/or to myself about how hard the exercises were. Anytime weight came up in conversation, I talked about how nothing I did made a difference, I complained and whined that I was working so hard and still couldn't lose weight. I was over 40 and everyone was telling me it was my age, or I had big bones or some other excuse that helped me feel I was doomed to stay this way. I was told my bulging abdomen was the result of my giving birth, and the only solution was a tummy tuck by plastic surgery. I looked in the mirror and told myself how fat I was; I stood in my closet and complained that nothing fit because I was so fat. I talked about my fat clothes; how clothes made me look fat. I would get angry and insulted and would strongly deny that my conversation was fat focused anytime someone else pointed out to me. I later discovered that my anger was my way of denying to myself that they were right.

Once I accepted what I was doing that might be adding to my weight problem, I wrote a list of what I could do that would make a positive change.

I found photos of myself from the past with the body and weight I wanted to be again, now. I put these pictures on my bathroom mirror, on my closet door and on my refrigerator. I carried a copy in my wallet. I wanted a visual reminder of what was once a reality and could possibly be again. I used Photoshop to edit some of my current photos so I looked my Ideal weight now. I looked at these photos everyday; obviously anytime I was in my bathroom, closet or kitchen. Next to the photo I wrote my Ideal weight and measurements. When I looked at the photos, I would then close my eyes and run my hands across my body, while seeing my Ideal body in my mind. When I would run my hands across my stomach, I would see a flat stomach in my mind and tell myself how happy I was to have a flat stomach. I reinforced the Ideal in my minds eye, my thoughts and my words.

When I started focusing on my Ideal body and listening to what my body wanted, I discovered that I didn't need a special diet. I focus on my Ideal body before going to the grocery store. I then write out my menu for a few days and only shop for those items.

I balanced my meal with good carbohydrates and protein. I quit drinking diet drinks and drank mineral water with juice instead. When I started to focus on my Ideal body for 1 minute before each meal I began to eat slower, ate smaller bites and tasted the food. Tasting the food has become a game to see if I could discern each individual flavor or seasoning. I did food experiments to see what I really did like and what was just an old habit. I found that pasta without sauce wasn't satisfying, but with the sauce it was really good. So this showed me that all the flavors I like were only in the sauce. Now I put the delicious sauce on foods I do like by themselves or with sauce, such as spinach, shredded carrots, broccoli and pureed cauliflower.

I am full every meal, I take the same amount of time for each meal as I used to and I am more satisfied.

When I go out to restaurants, I still Idealize my body before the meal to help me choose what I really want. I Idealize the perfect amount to eat and regardless of how much extra they bring on my plate, I only eat the portion I Idealized. I am no longer driven by cravings for junk food, processed sugar or fake sweeteners.

When I started paying attention to myself, I discovered that when I drove my car I slightly slumped back into the seat. Now I sit up straight and pull in my abdomen muscles. I relax my shoulders and I breathe. I drive much calmer.

On day I read that vitamin D is essential to good health and along with Calcium and Magnesium, and it was great for weight control. The best vitamin D is sunshine so he suggested 30 minutes each day exposing as much skin as possible without sunscreen. I never have enjoyed just laying in the sun, so I chose my legs to be the exposed skin and started walking around the block 30 minutes every few days with sunscreen only on my arms and face. I get vitamin D and a little sun color on my legs. I found a walking buddy with like-thinking, We walk in silence and we each focus on our Ideal body as we walk.

I discovered that when I took my walks around the neighborhood that I was swinging my arms but not really using any muscles in the process. I now walk with my ribcage when doing my walk workout and my arms are moved in the action.

I Idealize my muscles being toned and strong. I looked up the muscles structure on the internet so I could get a real grasp of which muscle I was focusing on. I poked my muscle with my finger, tightened it and released, so I could really focus on the specific muscle area. I talked with my personal trainer at the gym about my Ideal body and my muscle focus, so he works with me on my muscle focus and toning instead of just doing the same exercises he gives everyone else. I no longer watch TV when I exercise I look at pictures and home movies of my Ideal body.

My transformation was not without frustration as my old thoughts and habits weren't always easy to change. I relied on the Simple Keys to get me through those times. I used the Observe & Replace Key to help me change my words. I used the Worthiness Key to help me see how I did deserve the body I desired and recognize what fears were holding me back. I worked with a Life

Experience Coach who had similar experience to what I was going through. It helped me a lot to talk with someone who had been through it.

I now stand and sit taller and hold my stomach muscles in and now my lower back problems are also gone. I had been told for years that lower back and stomach muscles needed to balance each other. I finally got it. My normal walk has become a natural stride.

The hardest part was facing the truth about myself. I had the habit of denial. Once I took that step, made the changes I had always knew were necessary and used the Simple Keys and my Coaches to help me, I got the body I Idealized.

My first week, my body measured 1" smaller around my ribcage, ½" from waist and 3 pounds weight had melted away. Those results had not happened in the past with my old efforts and thinking.

At my 3 week mark, I was another 2" around my ribcage, another 1-1/2" from waist, and an additional 9 pounds had vanished.

After 2 months, my ribcage was another 3 " smaller, my waist was 7" smaller and 28 pounds are gone. I had heard in the past that those results could never happen that fast, but I did it, and I am healthy too.

My hunger is satisfied tastefully at every meal and I am recharged and full of energy. I can still eat lasagna, cookies, ice cream and some of my of my favorite treats. I now eat the Ideal amount and my hunger and body is more than satisfied. I sleep better and wake more rested. The results of my recent physical exam shoe all my vitals (blood pressure, stress, heart rate, cholesterol) are in excellent measures. I no longer have Type 2 Diabetes! Plus I measured a ½" taller in height.

Today, after 6 months, I still Idealize my perfect body so I can maintain my new habits and my healthy body without struggle. My weight has continued to drop away consistently and I am within a few pounds of my Ideal body. My friends tell me I look 10 years younger and even accuse me of having a face lift. My skin is clear and wrinkles have melted away with the unwanted inches." 11/01/07. ~ Shana Fazan, Milan, Wisconsin ~

How To Turn Your Desires and Ideals Into Reality

ATTAINING SPIRITUAL CONSCIOUSNESS AND CHANGING CHARACTER

How To Turn Your Desires and Ideals Into Reality

CHAPTER 27

PREVENTING MISTAKES IN THINKING

If you know how to prevent your mind making mistakes, that knowledge and the use of it will aid you in your advancement, stop failures in business, prevent friction in social life, stop the offending and losing of friends, and help very greatly in making you happier. Happiness is the goal of the soul. It is the end of human endeavor, the purpose of living and loving and serving.

How we have suffered because of the unintentional mistakes we have made! How we have made others suffer; how others have made us suffer! And not because of our intention or their intention, but because we did not know how to *Idealize* the process of

231

preventing mistakes. It is completeness that makes thought *Ideal* that makes it right, that makes it Divine Spiritual Source-like. Divine Spiritual Source is Divine Spiritual Source, because Divine Spiritual Source is complete, the perfect, the All-in-All. We make mistakes only when our thought is incomplete; that is, when it is not *Idealized*.

There are two factors in the process of thinking: (1) recognizing likenesses and (2) discriminating differences. If you *Idealize* the process of thinking, you complete it; you use both of these. If you do not *Idealize* the process, you use but one, or you use one almost to the exclusion of the other. And it is then that you make the mistakes that bring unhappiness.

A baby boy, reared in the tropics, was brought to New York when three years old. That winter as he looked out of the window at the first snow he had ever seen, he clapped his hands in glee and said, "Oh, mamma, look at all the sugar!" He recognized the likeness in appearance of snow and sugar, its whiteness, and he made the mistake because he had had no opportunity of distinguishing the differences.

A little girl, now a noted woman, was born in inland Peru in the nitrate section desert, an absolutely barren land where no vegetation could live. She had never seen grass; she had never seen a tree. When ten years old, she was taken by ship to Santiago and driven in a closed carriage through the city to the home of her grandfather. Out in the yard a few hours later, she saw a great tree. A breeze sprang up, the leaves rustled, the branches moved. In terror she picked up a stone to defend herself. To her, the tree was some gigantic animal making ready to attack her. She had never known a vegetable form of life that moved, for she had seen vegetables only in sacks and cans. But animals moved and since this tree moved, she judged it to be an animal. The mistake was based on the recognition of a likeness: animals move; this big thing moves; therefore it must be an animal.

Let me repeat: unintentional mistakes are caused by recognition of likenesses with insufficient discrimination of differences.

Another case, husband and wife and two young sons. The man has worked earnestly and efficiently, and his wife has helped. They are in comfortable circumstances. One son is in high school, the other in college. Oil is discovered in California west of the coast mountain ranges. The wells are gushing thousands of dollars worth of oil per day. The husband visits the desert lands east of the mountain range and, accidentally, in the crevices of a gully, he finds soaked chunks of earth that are oily. He feels of it; it feels oily. He looks at it; it looks oily. It feels and looks like the oil-soaked chunks of earth found in the oil region west of the mountains. In his mind, he sees oil gushers in this region like those west of the mountains. In his imagination he sees himself many times a millionaire like the men who discovered oil west of the mountains. As many know he is on this trip he does not confide his discovery to others. So he says nothing, but invests all his savings in this desert land. At the bank he borrows all he can borrow, to secure additional options. To this point, all his thought and action is based upon recognition of likenesses. Then the expert finds a difference. It looks like oil, but it is not oil. It feels greasy, just as petroleum feels greasy, but it is not petroleum. It is of no value.

It is so easy to see only likenesses. It is the lowest type of mind action. It is incomplete: It leads to mistakes. It brings unhappiness, so much unhappiness! To prevent mistakes in individual life, in home life, in business, in industrial and in national affairs *Idealize* the process of recognizing differences. *Idealize* your thoughts and your plans of action; whatever you are to do, *Idealize* the process. Sit quietly, vision the likenesses, do not omit them; but *Idealize* the differences also. *Idealize* the differences again and again, to be certain you include all of them. Only the *Idealized* process produces the *Ideal* result: happiness!

CHAPTER 28

OVERCOMING FORGETFULNESS AND IDEALIZING REMEMBERING

What a lot of personal, family, social and business troubles, yes, even tragedies, result from forgetfulness! You, and everyone, desire to change this mental habit of often and easily forgetting to a habit of remembering easily and readily. Such a habit of good memory cannot be attained by using the clownish mental gymnastics that are called "memory systems." Waste no time on these substitutes for memory. Many of their methods are ridiculous in nature and complex in operation. For instance, if you wish to remember who the Fourteenth

President of our country was, you are instructed to think of the initials of these two words F and P, and then to remember that it was Franklin Pierce. But F and P might also stand for "Filthy Pig!" Such a memory relationship would be of no value at all unless you had PREVIOUSLY remembered (1) that Franklin Pierce was the Fourteenth President; (2) that the initials of Franklin Pierce are F and P; (3) that the initials of the Fourteenth President are F and P; (4) that the initials of Franklin Pierce and Fourteenth President are the same; (5) that F and P must not be remembered as initials of Filthy Pig, Funny Pictures, False Policies, Fatty Peters, Fancy Poultry and (6) some 10,000 or more other possibilities of such initials.

To remember by using "memory systems" requires about ten times the energy and mind effort required by memory itself. It is when you have not remembered, that the mind makes effort. When you have remembered to do what you intended to do, the act of remembering was easy. Why? Because your mind then used its own process of remembering. If you *Idealize* this process, you make it perfect, a habit of remembering easily. What is the process of *Idealizing* memory? What is the mental act of *Idealizing* the process?

Let me make a confession. In my psychology, I wrote of this development of memory at least twenty years ago. I have used it much; I have never known it to fail when used. That is the point, when used.

A few months ago, after returning from Mexico and the south, I had no residence ready for me and for a few weeks took a place with which I was entirely unfamiliar, a place that was very inconvenient in that it was necessary to keep certain manuscripts in the basement. The electric lights of the basement were turned on by a button switch at the top of the stairs. I do not like to waste anything, yet for two weeks, over and over again, when I started for the basement I would find that the lights were already on. This meant that over and over again, after getting the important thing I wanted, I had forgotten to turn out the lights after I came up. I thought about this; I reminded myself again and again not to forget to turn out the lights; but my mind being occupied with things which I considered very much more important, I continued again and again to forget. This is the point: mere thinking to remember will not develop memory nor make you remember. A mere idea that you must remember something often leads to forgetfulness, no matter how good the intention to remember.

One day, like a flash it came to me that I had been very remiss in not putting my own *Ideals* into practice, the very things I had written twenty years ago, the very things I had practiced for twenty years whenever important things were to be remembered. What I did illustrates the *Idealizing* process. What you forget to do is not a material thing but the process in your mind that you intend to do a certain thing at a certain time. If you *Idealize* this process you build it into the structure so that it works automatically. This was the actual process I wished to attain.

I wished to be able automatically to go to the stair, even while my mind was centered upon getting important papers from the basement, turn on the lights, go down, get the papers, return, and automatically switch off the lights. As stated, I had previously thought of doing so, I had had an idea of doing so a score of times and had reproached myself for forgetting to do so.

It took two minutes to *Idealize* this process. I closed my eyes to shut out all other images. I first saw and then felt myself move, approaching the door leading to the basement; I saw and felt myself move in turning on the lights, descending the stairs, getting a file of papers, mounting the stairs, turning off the lights, and going about my work. Immediately I re-imaged this process. I went over it again; a third time; a fourth; a fifth.

What was the result?

That process was built automatically into my mind process. I had an *Ideal*, a perfect image of myself remembering to do the thing I wanted to do, built into the brain structure so that no matter how important were the things occupying my mind, I could go to the basement and return, not forgetting to turn out the lights, not even being bothered to remember to turn them out.

If your mind has been trained to *Idealize*, if it has been trained for only a week or a month, you can *Idealize* such a simple process fifty or a hundred times in five minutes, that is, if your eyes are closed so that the mind is not interrupted by impressions of other things.

Apply this *Idealized* process not only to memory, but to the development of any mental process you wish to establish, any habit of character you desire to attain. After all, memory is a habit of character, and the process given here, *Idealized* as I have described it, will change not only any mental process but any habit of character mental, ethical or spiritual. The essential thing is to *Idealize* the process, making it perfect in the mind; then it will always come true.

TESTIMONIAL:
5 MINUTES TO LOWER STRESS.

"After being a stay-at-home Mom for 18 years I finally landed a good assistant position in a large firm across town. Soon after I started this new job, I started to get consistent migraines. I was so concerned about forgetting something every time I left the house, and I worried about it all the way to work. When I had a migraine I had to stop everything and go to bed because I could no longer think, or move or do anything. I was afraid I might lose my new job. After being at home for so many years, I was afraid I might be forgetting to feed the pets, or turn something off, or forget to lock something on my rush to work. I read this book, and especially this chapter and the one about the doctor. It made sense enough that I decided to give it a try. Now before leaving my house to go to work, I take 5 minutes to Idealize myself comfortably driving to work with the feeling of confidence that I have completed everything at home; that everything that should be locked, is locked; everything that should be turned off , is off; the animals are fed, and so on; including that I am wearing the appropriate outfit to the office. I have been doing this now for 6 months, and have not had any of my usual stress migraines. My boss is happy that I no longer miss so many days from work and I find myself enjoying the drive to work listening to my favorite music instead of worrying." ~ Julie Cucina, San Francisco, CA ~

CHAPTER 29

CHANGING WEAK WILLS TO STRONG WILLS

What a tragedy it is to live with the will so weak that one cannot carry out that which one sincerely intends to do or live as one has conscientiously resolved to live. And, it is so easy, so very easy, to change what is called a weak will to a strong will if you *Idealize* the process that was used in the beginning to form the original intention or resolution. If you do this, the original intention with all its desire, is ever present and no effort is necessary to sustain the will. All success depends, however, upon the process being *Idealized*, being made perfect in the mind. In the case of will, the *Idealizing* applies most of all to *Idealizing* vivid images in the mind.

Will is the power that makes us persist in our efforts to carry out a decision long after the decision is made. A person with a weak will often makes a decision with the same good intention as one with a strong will, but the power to carry out their decision does not persist after a lapse of time because they cease to visualize the images that led them to make the decision in the first place.

Why does a person of good intentions, having made a promise in all sincerity, fail to keep it? Because of lack of will. Because they allow the images that led them to make the promise to become less vivid day by day. And as these images fade, as they become weaker and weaker, the individual leaves undone many things that should be done to enable them to keep the promise. A strong will keeps the images in mind day after day; a weak will permits them to fade. The decision at the time a promise is made is strong because the images, ideas and *Ideals* that lead one to make the decision are vivid at the time. If the images are kept vivid, the decision remains, and the will grows stronger instead of weaker.

<u>The case of a Boy and His Mother:</u> The boy is lovable, dutiful, obliging, sociable and *Ideal*istic, not a single bad habit. His mother is partly dependent upon him. He left the little Connecticut town to accept a position in New York City because the increased pay would make it possible for him to give more to his mother. Before leaving he vowed to himself and promised her that every Saturday night he would send her at least six dollars; that when his salary was increased he'd send her more.

<u>Failure Due to Weak Will</u>: The six dollars were sent the first, second, third, and fourth Saturday nights, but only five dollars were sent the fifth; and then the amount varied. Finally one Saturday night he had nothing to send; he did not even have enough to pay his room rent for the next week. He was just as lovable, obliging and *Ideal*istic as when he left home; but when he went out with the other office men to lunch he did not wish to seem miserly, so ordered what they ordered. When they invited him to join, then Dutch treat, at a good theatre, he went because he liked good entertainments. And so his

money was spent. His habits were still good, but his will was not strong enough to resist the temptation to spend money for the things of the city.

His Struggle: The night he was unable to send anything to his mother was a night of agony. He was not selfish, and, consequently, he suffered the more. He prayed, and he resolved, and he vowed that he'd never fail again. But, he did. Though he sent six dollars a week regularly for the four succeeding weeks, the seventh week he sent but four, and two of these he had borrowed.

How He Developed a Strong Will: He chummed with a fellow-worker in the office. One night the boy, in desperation, opened his heart to his friend, and the chum, who knew me, brought him to me. The boy felt his whole life would be a failure: "If I have not strength of will to resist these temptations, what will become of me when big ones come?"

The Process of _Idealizing:_ I asked him to close his eyes, to think of his home, to picture in his mind the house and the rooms in the house, to visualize his mother there, to visualize her love for him and his love for her; to visualize her needs, and how much the six dollars a week added to her comfort. That was all; there was to it.

"You now feel strong enough to keep your promise, do you not?" "Certainly," he replied, "I am strong enough now." "Then always keep this condition of the NOW with you; make it permanent in your mind; visualize, for fifteen minutes every morning and every night these same images of your mother's home, her needs, and the extra comforts your six dollars a week will provide. So long as these images are strong in your mind your will to keep your promise is strong. But when these images fade and the images of expensive lunches and theatres become stronger, your will to keep your promise becomes weak. To keep your will strong to keep the promise you made, _Idealize_ the images which led you to make the promise."

Twenty-four hours later he said over the telephone: "It's easy, desire to help mother is so strong I've not even a desire to waste money." And a year later he said the same thing, and he had lived up to it, too!

"If we did all the things we are capable of,

we would literally astound ourselves. "

~Thomas A. Edison ~

CHAPTER 30

NORMAL MEANS OF ATTAINING SPIRITUAL CONSCIOUSNESS

The race longs for spiritual development; the soul desires it. You have long held *Ideals* that you wish would come true. You have held *Ideals* that do not relate to the daily life, that do not relate to business or politics or world affairs; *Ideals* that are in addition to those of your home, your family, your friends; in other words, *Ideals* of your own spiritual consciousness; the desire to be at peace within yourself and at one with Divine Spiritual Source.

Spiritual consciousness completes life; it gives life the true balance, the balance of knowing both its actuality and its spirituality. Spiritual consciousness is a condition, a condition of being consciously in touch not only with all other souls but with Cosmic Consciousness, with Divine Spiritual Source, Divine Mind, God, The Infinite, Principle, anything you wish to name it. It is not recognition, nor acceptance, nor faith. It is not a thought of, nor about Divine Spiritual Source. It is consciousness, knowing Divine Spiritual Source. Certainly, I'd not write a word on how to attain spiritual consciousness if I thought you were looking for a means of attaining a sort of non-active state of etherealized super-holiness.

The aim of all religion and *Ideal*istic thought is to extend the scope of life; to get in closer touch with and be more responsive to The Infinite. This gives the keynote of the process by which we attain spiritual consciousness, making ourselves more responsive.

Responsiveness necessitates likeness, for only like qualities or conditions respond one to another. The vibration of one string of a violin produces a responsive vibration only in a string or wire or vibrating body capable of vibrating to a like note. Even seemingly contrasting people are drawn to each other by those qualities of soul that are common, although perhaps unconsciously common.

Intelligences of individuals differ much more than their love-natures. The ignorant peasant knows love as deep and pure and noble as the best-schooled man or woman of the world. Love is the great common denominator of Man and Divine Spiritual Source. Hence consciousness of love is the first step in attainment of spiritual consciousness.

But love's spiritual nature is not personal, hence the method must *Idealize* it; eliminate personality; use the process that has been *Idealized* in all the past for the three great unselfish manifestations of love: love of home, love of country, and love of Divine Spiritual Source. These have been most *Idealized* before the fire: the hearth-fire, the campfire, and the altar-fire.

No matter what the bickering of the day, the annoyances and disturbances, the disagreements, and perhaps even the quarrels, they all disappear when the family gathers about the open hearth-fire. Little by little conversation ceases, which means that thought ceases, and the vague consciousness of love permeates each, taking each in his reveries to the very borderland of spiritual consciousness. So also around the campfire of the army.

No matter what the friction of the day between officers and men, or the discontent, or the horrors of the struggle, they disappear, and the same vague consciousness of love quiets the men, and takes them also to the borderland.

And the same is true, perhaps to a greater extent, before the altar-fire. One cannot attain spiritual consciousness by thinking. Thinking is mind activity; the mind reaches out into all the world in search of new impressions and new ideas to be taken within itself and treasured up for its own use. Its activity is toward the self, therefore selfish.

Love is emotion, it is a moving out, and its nature is to give. Its activity is away from the self, therefore un-self-ish. Unselfishness is not attained by selfishness. Therefore thinking, thought, or thought affirmations will not awaken a consciousness of love. Moreover, thinking, thought and thought affirmations prevent the attainment of spiritual knowing and establish instead thoughts about spiritual consciousness.

The first step, then, is to quiet thought; the second, to awaken love by the most *Idealized* process of all the ages, and that is *Idealization* before the fire. You know the effects whether before the open-fire in the home or the campfire in the woods. First, you cease to think, conversation lags, then stops, and the body relaxes. Second, daily troubles vanish, and a kindly attitude and an indefinite contentment come to you; Third, there comes not a conscious but a super-conscious condition, beginning with reverie; and then all thought ceases, and since all thought has ceased you are not even conscious that it has ceased; until, Fourth, with a start, you come back to yourself, that is, back to mental consciousness. But you have been on the borderland of spiritual consciousness.

Continued, before the open-fire, impersonally the most *Idealized* process of all times, the super-conscious state soon becomes illuminated and spiritual consciousness is attained. Awakened in this way, it does not unfit one for the daily work of life; it becomes the balance; the proper balance of Cosmic Realization and Practical Life.

"Under the law of nature, all persons are born free, every one comes into the world with a right to his own person, which includes the liberty of moving and using it at his own will. This is what is called personal liberty."
~ Thomas Jefferson ~

How To Turn Your Desires and Ideals Into Reality

Simple Key – Mindfulness

Achieving and maintaining your *Ideal* requires practicing Mindfulness in your daily life.

What is Mindfulness?

mindfulness, noun , dictionary.com
1. the trait of staying aware; paying close attention
2. Attentive; heedful

Mindfulness is being fully present, in each moment of your life, and being aware in all your choices, opinions, judgments and experiences. As you *Idealize* your desire, Mindfulness is listening to your inner voice, your body signals and using this information to consciously make your choices.

Mindfulness is being aware of "why" you do the things you do and choosing to do the same or make conscious changes. Mindfulness is listening and paying attention to the answers, when you ask "How" can I have things different in my life?

Mindfulness is being willing to stop, think and question the premature cognitive commitments you made early in life and your habits. As you *Idealize* your desires, you will be challenged to make changes in your actions.

> *"The definition of insanity is*
> *continuing the same thoughts and behaviors*
> *and expecting different results."*
> *~ Albert Einstein ~*

Mindfulness is marching to your own tune, accepting that you are in control of when and how you do things;

RESPONDing rather than REACTing to life and living from choice rather than from fear.

"The highest manifestation of life consists in this:
that a being governs its own actions.
A thing which is always subject to the direction of
another is somewhat of a dead thing. "
~ Saint Thomas Aquinas ~

QUOTES
AND
REFERENCES

Albert Schweitzer, M.D., OM,

(1875 – 1965)

An Alsatian theologian, musician, philosopher, and physician. He challenged both the secular view of historical Jesus current at his time and the traditional Christian view, depicting a Jesus who expected the imminent end of the world. In 1953, he received the 1952 Nobel Peace Prize for his philosophy of "reverence for life".

Brendan Francis Behan

(1923 - 1964)

An Irish poet, short story writer, novelist and playwright who wrote in both English and Irish. He was one of the most successful Irish dramatists of the 20th century.

St. Thomas Aquinas

(1225 –1274)

An Italian Catholic priest in the Dominican Order, a philosopher and theologian in the scholastic tradition. He was the foremost classical proponent of natural theology, and the father of the Thomistic school of philosophy and theology.

Aristotle

(384 BC – 322 BC)

A Greek philosopher, a student of Plato and teacher of Alexander the Great. He wrote on many different subjects, including physics, metaphysics, poetry, theater, music, logic, rhetoric, politics, government, ethics, biology and zoology. He was one of the most important philosophers in Western thought, and was one of the first to systematize philosophy and science. His thinking on physics and science had a profound impact on medieval thought, which lasted until the Renaissance, and the accuracy of some of his biological observations was only confirmed in the last century.

Henry David Thoreau

(1817 –1862)

An American author, naturalist, transcendentalist, development critic, and philosopher. Public figures like Mahatma Gandhi, President John F. Kennedy, Martin Luther King, Jr., Supreme Court Justice William O. Douglas, and author Leo Tolstoy, and many others all spoke of being strongly affected by Thoreau's work.- -

William James

(1842 –1910)

A pioneering American psychologist and philosopher. He wrote influential books on the young science of psychology, educational psychology, psychology of religious experience and mysticism. He was godson of Ralph Waldo Emerson. He spent his entire academic career at Harvard studying medicine, physiology, and biology, and although he taught in those subjects, he was drawn to the scientific study of the human mind at a time when psychology was constituting itself as a science.

Orison Swett Marden

(1850 - 1924)

An American writer, with a degree in medicine, a successful hotel owner and founder of Success Magazine, is also considered to be the founder of the modern success movement in America. He believed that our thoughts influence our lives and our life circumstances. His large body of written material has helped countless thousands of people the world over to come into a better understanding of the principles of prosperity and success. Although he is best known for his books on financial success, he always emphasized that this would come as a result of cultivating one's personal development.

Sumner Davenport

(1951-   )

She is sought after as a speaker and she is quoted often. One of Sumner's quotes was voted to be included in the **Top 10 Healthy Thoughts of 2007.** She can be reached through her website:

www.sumnerdavenport.com

Georg Wilhelm Friedrich Hegel

(1770 –1831)

A German philosopher and one of the representatives of German *Ideal*ism. In his works he discussed a relation between nature and freedom, immanence and transcendence, and the unification of these dualities without eliminating either pole or reducing it to the other. His books describe his account of the evolution of consciousness from sense-perception to absolute knowledge and the logical and metaphysical core of his philosophy.

James Allen

(1864 - 1912)

A British philosophical writer known for his inspirational books and poetry. His belief insists upon the power of the individual to form his own character and to create his own happiness; the outer conditions of a person's life will always be found to be harmoniously related to his inner state. Allen's books illustrate the use of the power of thought to increase personal capabilities. His works continue to influence people around the world. His most famous book, *As a Man Thinketh*, published in 1902, is now considered a classic self-help book.

Napoleon Hill

(1883-1970)

An American author was one of the earliest producers of the modern genre of personal-success literature. His most famous work, *Think and Grow Rich*, is the all time bestseller in the field. In America, Hill stated in his writings, people are free to believe what they want to believe, and this is what sets the United States apart from all other countries in the world. Hill's works examined the power of personal beliefs, and the role they play in personal success. "What the mind of man can conceive and believe, it can achieve" is one of Hill's hallmark expressions.

Gaston Bachelard
(1884 –1962)

A French philosopher who rose to some of the most prestigious positions in the French academy. His most important work is on poetics and the philosophy of science. He influenced many French philosophers in the latter part of the twentieth century.

Kathleen Mansfield
(1888 –1923)

A prominent New Zealand modernist writer of short fiction widely considered one of the best short story writers of her period.

Carlos Castaneda

(1932 – 1998)

A Peruvian or Brazilian-born American author. He wrote a series of books that describe his training in traditional Mesoamerican shamanism. He often referred to this unknown realm as nonordinary reality, which indicated that this realm was indeed a reality, but radically different from the ordinary reality experienced by human beings who are well engaged in everyday activities as part of their social conditioning.

Frederick Douglass

(1818 –1895)

An American abolitionist, editor, orator, author, statesman and reformer. He is one of the most prominent figures in African American history and a formidable public presence. He was a firm believer in the equality of all people.

Pierre Teilhard de Chardin

(1881 -1955)

A French philosopher and Jesuit priest who trained as a paleontologist and geologist and took part in the discovery of Peking Man. His primary book, The Phenomenon of Man, set forth a sweeping account of the unfolding of the cosmos on which he abandoned traditional interpretations of creation in the Book of Genesis in favor of a less strict interpretation. His work was denied publication during his lifetime by the Roman Catholic Church officials, however, Pope John XXIII rehabilitated him posthumously, and, since then, his works have been considered an important influence on the contemporary church's stance on evolution.

Thomas Edison

(1847-1931)

Edison is considered one of the most prolific inventors in history, holding 1,093 U.S. patents in his name, as well as many patents in the United Kingdom, France and Germany. Edison's greatest contribution was the first practical electric lighting. He not only invented the first successful electric light bulb, but also set up the first electrical power distribution company. Edison invented the phonograph, and made improvements to the telegraph, telephone and motion picture technology. He also founded the first modern research laboratory.

Henri Paul Gauguin

(1848 –1903)

A leading Post-Impressionist painter. His bold, colorful and design oriented paintings significantly influenced Modern art.

Thomas Jefferson

(1743 –1826)

The third President of the United States (1801–1809), the principal author of the Declaration of Independence (1776), and one of the most influential Founding Fathers for his promotion of the *Ideals* of Republicanism in the United States. As a political philosopher, Jefferson was a man of the Enlightenment also achieving distinction as, among other things, a horticulturist, statesman, architect, archaeologist, paleontologist, author, inventor and founder of the University of Virginia.

Albert Einstein

(1879-1955)

German-born theoretical physicist, best known for his theory of relativity and specifically mass-energy equivalence, $E = mc2$. Einstein received the 1921 Nobel Prize in Physics; In 1999 Einstein was named Time magazine's "Person of the Century", and a poll of prominent physicists named him the greatest physicist of all time. Today, the name "Einstein" has become synonymous with genius

About The Authors

Landone Brown

(1847-1945)

Brown Landone was one of the first teachers of the scientific understanding of accomplishments.

He was born into a wealthy family in Philadelphia, and was always known as a sickly child who had to be nursed through one illness after another and he lived the usual routine of an invalid. When he was about thirteen, his life changed dramatically after a frightening event. Left alone while his caretakers were on an errand, he became aware that the house had broken out in fire. Landone was virtually helpless by many medical accounts at that point in his frail life; however, he remembered his father had a metal chest in the attic which held all the valuable family papers. It was essential that this metal chest survive the fire.

Moments later Landone was found on the sidewalk with the heavy metal chest at his side. No one seemed to question how he and the metal chest got from the attic and down 5 floors to the street. Landone knew his subconscious mind had somehow made it happen, without his conscious awareness of it He reasoned that if he could do that subconsciously when he was ill, he certainly could do it consciously. At age 17 he was diagnosed by Doctors as having a critically defective heart which would kill him in a few months. Following some of the processes stated in this book, Landone went to his follow-up examination 2 years later and the same doctors diagnosed his heart as perfectly healthy.

He was always spiritually minded even though he was academically and scientifically educated. He was educated by private tutors, later studied for the ministry in England and received a Doctor of Divinity degree He studied and received a degree in medicine. In his medical practice he learned how the mind and conscious *Idealizing* aided his patients in healing, sometimes better than traditional medicine. He became known as one of the first psychiatrists through his work in localization of brain centers. He was an international historian, educator, author and writer of many books and courses. Many thousands have been helped by his powerful writings.

Dr. Brown Landone lived to the splendid age of 98. His life was full of accomplishments, including: He was President of the International Committee on New Education, which included 100 of the greatest educators in 17 countries. He was Editor-in-Chief of a "History of Civilization" with other noted educators. Throughout the early 1900's he lectured at renowned Universities, such as Oxford University in England and the Sorbonne in Paris.

After a research tour in Germany, he predicted the start of the First World War; was appointed by the President of France as a special ambassador for France to the United States; discovered hidden items in reports of the Japanese government, which showed they were then using school funds to build submarines secretly;

and he exposed the method by which the German Imperial Government made state socialism appear profitable.

He was also consultant to sales managers of Ford Motor Company, U. S. Steel, and Metropolitan Life.

After losing his three sons as a result of war casualties, Landone turned his interest to the promotion of Peace. He was instrumental in forming a European Peace Foundation. His quote tells much about his philosophy: "There will never be continuing peace on earth until a transformation is wrought by LOVE in the heart of man."

When silent movies were changing to talking movies he was called to Hollywood to help fit the voice to microphone and the microphone to the voice.

He carried on many experiments with an Asian shrub, Ramie, a fiber used in textiles. His demonstrations were attended by prominent people from all over the United States. The Landone Foundation, founded by Dr. Landone, conducted an experimental farm in Zellwood and successfully grew Ramie in large quantities.

About The Contributing Author

Sumner M. Davenport

(1951-)

Sumner Davenport is a woman with an unquenchable thirst for knowing the answers to life. Her deepest passion is to see people reach their full potential and achieve the life of their dreams while helping others to do the same.

Sumner believes it is important to be consciously active in making positive changes in our world. She has received acknowledgement from the Child Advocates office of the Los Angeles Superior Court, for her "Outstanding Service to Children", as a Court Appointed Special Advocate (CASA) Guardian ad Litem. For several years Sumner has been invited to conduct facilitator training to the students who organize the annual Conejo Valley Future Foundations' Youth Congress. Sumner dedicates a significant effort to the marketing and promotion of The Lorraine Jackson Foundation/Pearls of Hope® non-profit corporation and to 23rd Street Station philanthropic organization. Sumner participated in the Vancouver 26.2 mile Marathon to help raise funds and awareness for The Wellness Community.

Sumner credits her best education to the University of Hard Knocks, with crash courses in *taking risks* and advanced learning from *bouncing back*.

She facilitates Mindful meditation groups and has co-authored several books. She is sought after as a speaker and she is quoted often. One of Sumner's quotes was voted to be included in the **Top 10 Healthy Thoughts of 2007.**

She is also known for her trademark quote:

*The **INVESTMENTS** we make in ourselves,*
always deliver the most profitable returns. ™

She can be reached through her website:

www.sumnerdavenport.com

Facebook page:

https://www.facebook.com/sumner.davenport

Amazon Author Profile:

http://www.amazon.com/Sumner-M.-Davenport

Testimonial Contributors:

Note: As the internet grows, people change locations and email addresses, we cannot guarantee that the contact information below is always current.

I Finally Understood the Difference, Terry Bessel, Austin, TX, TMBessel7998@aol.com

I Wasn't Worthy to Have What I Desired~ *SPB, Orange, CA,~ Name & e-Mail Withheld by Request.*

My Best Sale Ever, Arthur Mansfield, Palo Alto, California, Arthur_mnsfld@yahoo.com

I Got My *Ideal* **Home**, Karen Moore, Woodland Hills, California, karenmoore01ana_stuart@yahoo.com

Finally Getting My Ideal Body, Shana Fazan, Milan, Wisconsin, shanaf@usa.com

5 Minutes To Lower Stress, Julie Cucina, San Francisco, California, juliecucina@sanfranmail.com

As we continue to bring some of the inspiration and educational works from enlightened masters of the past back into print we seek current testimonials to support these messages. If you follow the messages and tools introduced in these books and have a testimonial of success you would like to share, please send us an email:

books@selfinvestmentpublishing.com

Recommended Reading

There are many teachers and tools to assist you in living the life of your dreams. We all learn from different teachers and different delivery of the message.

The following is a short list of books and authors which may assist you in finding your answers:

It Works with Simple Keys - Jarrett/Davenport

The Miracle of Mindfulness – Thich Nhat Hahn

Think and Grow Rich – Napoleon Hill

Practicing The Power of Now – Eckhart Tolle

The Hidden Messages in Water –Masaru Emoto

The Greatest Salesman in the World – Og Mandino

An Essay on Concentration – Ralph Waldo Emerson

Power vs. Force: The Hidden Determination of Human
    Behavior – David R. Hawkins

A Separate Reality – Carlos Castaneda

Radical Forgiveness – Colin Tipping

Illusions, the Adventures of a Reluctant Messiah
    – Richard Bach

Recommended Reading

No Ordinary Moments – Dan Millman

The Celestine Prophecy: An experimental Guide

   – James Redfield & Carol Adreinne

The Fantasy Bond – Robert W. Firestone, Ph.D.

Begin it Now – Susan Hayward

The Body Reveals – Ron Kurtz & Hector Prestera, M.D.

Spirit at Work, Discovering the Spirituality in Leadership

   – Jay Conger & Associates

Synchronicity, the Inner Path of Leadership

   – Joseph Jaworski

Dhammapada, the Sayings of the Buddha

Creating True Prosperity – Shakti Gawain

Motivation & Personality – Abraham H. Maslow

The Law of Psychic Phenomena

   – Thomas J. Hudson, PhD

These and many other recommendations can be ordered through our websites:

http://astore.amazon.com/selfinvestment-20

ADDITIONAL RESOURCES:

"We must also be careful to avoid ingesting toxins
in the form of violent TV programs, video games, movies,
magazines, and books.
When we watch that kind of violence,
we water our own negative seeds, or tendencies,
and eventually we will think and act out of those seeds."
~ Thich Nhat Hahn ~

- a cinematic journey of the heart, mind & spirit.
- Awaken your sense of joy and wonder!
- Inspire love and compassion!
- Evoke a deeper sense of connection
with everything that is important around you!

www.MoviesWithMessages.com

GIVING BACK

...all things are possible

The Lorraine Jackson Foundation

The Foundation's primary mission is to provide scholarships for secondary education for children who have lost a parent to breast cancer.

The Foundation, through Pearls of Hope®, raises money by the generous donations from individuals, corporate and foundation sponsorships, online fundraising partnerships, an annual Golf Classic and the annual Pearls of Hope Awards and Scholarship Gala.

www.PearlsofHope.com

The Lorraine Jackson Foundation
1925 Century Park East, Suite 800
Los Angeles, Ca. 90067
(310) 753-6556

Pearls of Hope® is a registered trademark of The Lorraine Jackson Foundation, a California 501(c)(3) non-profit organization.

CASA
Court Appointed Special Advocates

GIVE A CHILD A VOICE

In the United States over one half million children are in foster care because they cannot safely live with their families. Nearly 70,000 National CASA volunteers serve approximately 280,000 of those abused or neglected children every year.

www.casaforchildren.org

SELF INVESTMENT COMPANY

"May you always have work for your hands to do.
May your pockets hold always a coin or two.
May the sun shine bright on your window pane.
May the rainbow be certain to follow each rain.
May the hand of a friend always be near you.
And may Spirit fill your heart
with gladness to cheer you."
~ Irish Blessing~

SELF-INVESTMENT COMPANY, LLC © 2007
2060d E. Avenida de los Arboles #571
Thousand Oaks, CA 91362

Made in the USA
Las Vegas, NV
22 November 2020